Growing Up Rural

You Smell Barn

Janet Letnes Martin

and

Suzann (Johnson) Nelson

CARAGANA PRESS

CARAGANA PRESS
BOX 274
HASTINGS, MN 55033

Printed in the United States of America

Published by Caragana Press
PO Box 274, Hastings, MN 55033

Library of Congress Cataloging-in-Publication Data
Library of Congress Control Number is pending.

ISBN: 1-886627-16-9

FIRST EDITION

Cover Design: Graphic Design, Inc.
                    Hastings, MN

Printer: Sentinel Printing
                    (A division of Bang Printing)
                    St. Cloud, MN

In Memory of Deloyd Johnson
1933 — 2014

The guy who...

- knew more about tractors than anyone else, and
- loved classical choral music, and
- knew more Ole and Lena jokes than anyone else, and
- was a Lutheran, but still danced better than Lawrence Welk, and
- attended all our "Church Basement Musicals," and
- bought Twinkies for our adult daughters, and
- laughed at us, but most of all,
- *MADE US LAUGH !*

Contents

Introduction

"Vini, Vidi, Vici"
They Came, They Saw,
They Conquered

Times were tough in the old countries, and diseases and crop failures took their toll on the people. Those that knew how to work, weren't in line to inherit the farm, and thought that pastors were getting too highbrow for their own good, thought "enough is enough," and left.

With a wooden trunk in hand, they shook hands with the old folks, bought a ticket in steerage class on a steamer, and landed in Canada or Ellis Island with dreams of making it to the Midwest to have their own farm.

Within days after they arrived at their destination (usually at a relative's home), they immediately started working for "board and keep." They supplemented their incomes by working on the railroad, or in the Northwoods chopping trees to save up money for their own homestead. As soon as they had saved up enough to get by, they went to a local land office and plunked down $18.00 for a 160-acre homestead. They signed off that they were at least 21 years, would work the land for five years, build a house and had made plans to apply for citizenship.

They worked from sunup to sundown clearing the land. They loaded rocks on stone-boats, blasted tree stumps out of the earth, tilled the soil with oxen, planted trees, hauled the water and hauled the wood. They choked on soot coming from sod houses and prairie fires, and they sweat like butchers.

Our people came to farm the land that was located in the heart of the Midwest; the states of Minnesota, North Dakota, South Dakota, Wisconsin and Iowa. Within these five states were 377 counties with hundreds and hundreds of small towns and thousands of townships that were dotted with lakes, land, farmsteads, churches and schools.

We didn't count the Midwest to include states such as Montana and Wyoming because they had too many cowboys, or Midwest states such as Nebraska and Kansas because they were too far south to know what winter was all about. Indiana and Illinois didn't count as Midwest states because the southern part of those states didn't speak our same language. We didn't count the whole state of Michigan as being a Midwest state because geographically we thought most of it was located too far "out East" to qualify. So, we lumped the Finns who lived in the northwest part of Michigan in with their counterparts who lived in Wisconsin, and called it good enough.

Immigrants from Norway tried to claim plots of land that didn't look like it was chocked-full of rocks and other obstacles. The Danish immigrants were not as driven as the Norwegians. They liked to "stop and smell the roses," and were thankful for any kind of land.

Swedish immigrants looked for land that was near lakes and water. They, unlike the Norwegians, needed some free time to fish and to sit by the lake and think of things such as how they could train a swallow to bring a greeting back home to their people in Dalarna.

Finnish immigrants had a little "dark side" to them and would look for land by forests and rivers so they could hide out and cleanse their bodies and minds. In the dead of winter, they religiously would sit bare-naked in a hot sauna shack until they sweat so badly they just about passed out.

Sometimes they would up the ante and beat themselves with birch branches to really do it up. After they felt woozy from the heat, they would roll in the snow butt-naked, and finish by jumping into a hole in the frozen lake. Finnish immigrants were normal during the rest of the seasons.

German immigrants were a mixed bag. Some were Lutheran and some were Catholic, but it didn't much matter to them where they homesteaded. They just tried to hog the best land. Sometimes they succeeded, but sometimes the Norwegians beat them to it. The Irish immigrants were Catholic and knew how to jig, use the jigger, and celebrate anything. They looked for land that was located in close proximity to a small town.

Rural by Luck

Farms began to sprout up all over the landscape, and most of them took on the appearances of mini-towns. Buildings on a farm would oftentimes grow to include: a cow barn, pole barn, loafing barn, farrowing barn and turkey barn; a homestead house, pump house, milk house, well house, engine house, brooder house, bunk house, summer kitchen house and an outhouse; the grease shed, tool shed, wood shed, shearing shed and machine shed. In addition, farmsteads had Quonset huts, Butler bins, potato warehouses, corn cribs, granaries, sheep pens, lean-tos, trench silos and a milking parlor.

The farmyards, pastures and machine sheds were homes to pickups, tractors, trucks, combines, Caterpillars, plows, disks, diggers, swathers, binders, cultivators, tillers, sprayers and other types of machinery that were used to farm the land. The groves of trees that were part of the landscape were used as a resting place for rusted out threshing machines, and other machinery that had bit the dust.

The "White House"

Most farmhouses had two stories, a basement, a storm cellar, and one or two porches that were usually enclosed after a remodeling job. They were painted white, and after some time, most were in need of a good paint job.

The yard was full of shade trees, weeping willows and Russian olive trees. It was bordered by lilac bushes, and Caragana and honeysuckle hedges. In the summer, the houses were framed by hollyhocks, petunias and other flowers, and banked in the winter with tarpaper and hay bales. A large vegetable garden was located nearby.

The kitchen was the center of the universe in a farm home. It was the place where cooking, canning, eating, visiting and reciting Confirmation memory work to parents was done. The living room was usually a little more spiffed up and was used at Christmas time, when company came to visit and a place to entertain homemakers' club. Some farmhouses had a dining room that was only used for dining at Christmas, Easter or for Confirmation meals. The dining room often doubled as a sewing room or as a place to park the piano.

Furniture in the house was practical, sensible and wasn't replaced until it was really worn out, or the kids had moved out. Art that was hung on our walls included a picture of *The Gleaners, The Lone Wolf, Grace, The Lord's Supper,* an aerial shot of the farm with its surrounding shelterbelts, and high school graduation photos of the kids.

A reminder to work hard

A reminder to be thankful

**A reminder to pay attention
to dangers that were lurking**

The bedrooms and storeroom were located upstairs, and most bedrooms were shared with siblings. An extra bathroom was sometimes added upstairs in the homes when "Modern Housekeeping" was put in place.

Many houses had a dirt cellar instead of a basement. A farmhouse basement basically looked like a dungeon with multi-rooms that served multi-purposes. It housed the deep freezer, milk separator and a big sink to clean off barn smells. It contained an area either for a coal bin, oil tanks and a furnace. It had a separate room called a fruit cellar, even though most of the canning that was done wasn't fruit, but pickles and vegetables. An area was carved out of the basement for washing and wringing out clothes. Makeshift clothes lines were set up for winter use. Most farm basements were poorly lit, and had a pretty good-sized mouse population.

The "welcome mat" was a manure scrapper which was located by the door. Front doors were outfitted with a lock that could be opened or locked with a skeleton key. However, front doors were never locked because nobody ever knew where the skeleton key was located.

The Barn – The "Castle" on the Farm

Out of necessity, the barn was oftentimes the first building built on a homestead, even before the house. It was built by a crew, not a crane. If it was destroyed by a fire or a tornado, the neighbors came together and held a "barnraising" for the unlucky farmer, and the women cooked the meals for the crew.

The barn, with its silo, was the "castle" on the farm. Everyone knew that the bigger the barn, the more prestigious and prosperous the farmer. No matter the size of the barns, they all had the same distinct odor. The smell of barn was a combination of manure, rancid milk and silage. It penetrated any person and the clothes that they were wearing who walked into a barn, and it clung to them and to their clothes when they left the barn.

It was more than a building to house cows, horses, oxen, sheep, fowl, dogs, cats, mice, spiders, flies and birds of all kinds. The barn symbolized the farmer's main bank. The animals not only provided food for the family, but wool for clothing, and feather's for mattresses. From the sale of eggs and cream, the Mrs. was able to purchase staples that couldn't be raised in the barn or grown in the fields.

The barn was also the "homestead hospital," the building where the farmers attended to the animals' births and deaths. The rendering trucks backed up to pick up the dead. Tragically, it was also the place where some of the homesteaders or their offspring hung themselves on ropes when they couldn't take it anymore.

All barns had their own stories, and if barn walls could talk, they would tell of kids smoking cigarettes for the first time behind the barn, and of young bucks trying to get girls to "roll in the hay" in the hayloft. It was a place where tramps, bums and some hired men were found passed out with their empty bottles of cheap liquor littered around them.

The second story in the barn was the place where hay was stored, and where kids played, jumped and swang on ropes. In the summer before the new hay was loaded in, kids used the space to practice basketball. It was also a Sanctuary City for cats that needed to carve out a place to hide while giving birth.

Many barns were painted red in honor of an early tradition, and many had second stories that were laid with maple wood floors. When a barn was no longer used to house animals (except for birds on the cupola, skunks and cats), they were sometimes turned into a place to store machinery or a place to hold barn dances. Eventually, many of them became bygone monuments and were left to collapse with their faded peeling paint, broken windows, busted doors and rusted door hinges. The smell of barn lingered until a barn was plowed under, and the only memories left were photographs.

*The Egg
Money Bank*

Home of the Easter Ham

The Granary

The granary was the farmer's back-up bank. Grain was stored until a farmer sold it or used it as feed for the livestock. (In the '40s and the first half of the '50s, farmers couldn't count on the Soil Bank to bring in extra cash.) Kids were warned to never play in the granary, but most of them did. Many have memories of panicking while sinking into the flax or wheat. Granaries were also a place where bodies were "wintered over" until the ground at the cemetery thawed enough to dig the bodies six feet under. Skunks usually hung out by the granary, and sprayed when they were annoyed or felt threatened.

Norwegian by Birth

Many of our Norwegian ancestors came from the same valleys and areas in the old countries and settled down in the same districts and areas in the Midwest. Brothers from one family married sisters from another family, and double cousins became the norm. Eventually most of them became shirt-tail relatives. By the time a few generations had passed, "Your people shall be my people" went the way of the threshing machine. Some married outside their ethnic heritages, some outside their counties and townships, and some found helpmeets that lived in town and were of English and other non-Scandinavian descent. And, "Your God shall be my God," was put to the test when some even married outside their faith. After a few decades, most people didn't know who begat whom and how they were related until there was a jubilee celebration in the area and someone figured it out for them.

In the township's beginning, who to marry got a little tricky. There wasn't much choice. This is perhaps portrayed best in *"The Urness Genealogy Challenge" in the book, The History of Urness Township, 135 Years of Rural Community Life,* compiled and published in 2004 by the Urness Township (MN) History Committee.

The Urness Genealogy Challenge

Erick Thorson (Thoreson), 1850-1933, was already twice a widower with five children — Nels, Albert, Martin, John and Ida — when he married Bothilda (Thue) Urness, the widow of Ole J. Urness. Bothilda was the mother of twelve children: Martha, Carrie, John, Louisa, Louis, Onne, Bennie, Andrew, Emma, Mary, Annie and Olena. All became stepchildren of Erick Thorson. Bothilda died after only a few years of marriage to Erick, and all of the children and stepchildren then had to live with relatives or on their own.

Soon Erick Thorson married again. His fourth wife, Mary (Underdahl) Thue, was the widow of Erick Thue and Bothilda's sister-in-law. Mary had seven children: Mathilda, Robert, Selma, Luella, Andrew, Isabelle and Elmer. The Thue stepchildren were already first cousins of the Thorson Urness stepchildren, and to complicate matters further, Erick's children began to intermarry. Albert Thorson married his stepsister, Emma Urness, Bennie Urness married his stepsister, Ida Thorson; and Andrew Urness married his stepbrother Nels' daughter, Emma Thorson.

Therefore, some of Emma Thorson Urness's aunts and uncles also became her sisters-in-law and brothers-in-law. Stepbrothers Albert and Bennie became double brothers-in-law, and stepsisters Emma Urness Thorson and Ida became double sisters-in-law. Emma Thorson became Emma Urness, and Emma Urness became Emma Thorson. In order to clarify things, the neighbors fondly referred to them as Big Emma and Little Emma, based on their height. Erick's fifth wife was a mail-order bride, but she left shortly after she arrived.

Lutheran by Golly

Shortly after townships were platted, the Norwegian immigrants built their churches, and called their pastors. The churches were identical in structure, the steeples were the same height, and the women were the driving forces behind the churches. The Swedes and Danes in the townships had no intentions of sitting in the same pews as the Norwegians, so they built their own Lutheran churches.

Lutheran pastors preached on sin and damnation, and officiated at baptisms, confirmations, weddings and burials. Most Lutheran pastors were somber, stern and intimidating. Pastors' wives were treated as special and were never expected to put their hands in a dishpan full of water. The women were the ones who did the majority of the work to keep the churches running and the doors open. The men worked a little on the buildings and grounds and were in charge of the cemeteries, ushering and hauling the women who didn't drive to Ladies Aid meetings.

It didn't take long before infighting started in

Scandinavian congregations all across the Midwest. Some people longed for the "high church" and thought their pastors needed to wear robes and large pleated collars like they did in Norway, Sweden and Denmark. Other people, the "low church" people, wanted their pastor to ditch the robes and all the garb and wear a suit like everyone else did in the congregation.

One issue in the early 20th century that split many Lutheran congregations had to do with the Biblical interpretation of predestination. Some thought the Bible taught we were saved by grace, and others thought you just couldn't use that as an excuse and go on sinning and think grace alone was going to save you. Then there were those like the Presbyterians who thought that you were predestined, and no matter what you did to make it right, it wasn't your call.

When members of a congregation couldn't agree, they split off and started a new congregation. As the years went by new Lutheran churches opened, and old Lutheran churches closed in townships and counties across the nation. The art of splitting and merging took hold and never lost its grip in the Lutheran churches in America. Over time Lutherans have belonged to the ALC, ELC, LFC, LCA, AALC, EFCA, TALC, LCMS, AFLC, ULCA, ELS. ELCA, LCR, LCS, CLC, CLBA, ALCA, ACLC. The only way we could all be in union is if we formed the AFL-CIO – The American Federation of Lutherans Coerced into One.

Part I
In the Beginning...
God Created Fish County

Viking Township

In the beginning God created Fish County, the county where Viking Township was located. Fish County included many townships, eight small towns, and the county seat, Otter Falls. Along with stores, Otter Falls had a train depot, and two intersections with signal lights.

Townships formed the basic structure of a rural community. Each contained 36 sections of land, and each section was six miles by six miles. These included roads, lakes, sloughs and rivers. Viking Township was settled by Norwegians, some Swedes and Germans, and a few Finns. The Norwegians, Swedes and Germans had arrived in the 1860s through the 1880s and cleared the land. Later, about 1915, the Finns began to arrive.

Originally, Viking Township was homesteaded by Johnsons, Olsons, Nelsons, Petersons, Carlsons, Andersons, Urnesses, Letnesses, Barsnesses, Petersens, Gundersons, Schmidts, Schneiders, Schultzes, Bauers, Wagners, Ahos, Erkillas, Haapalas and Jokinens.

The Finns were found mostly in the southeast corner of the township, and the Germans and other ethnic groups were scattered around.

Along with farms, most townships had a few churches and cemeteries, one or two one-room schoolhouses that were in the

process of consolidating with a town school, and a township hall. Organizations were formed or expanded, and meetings were held in the township hall or sometimes the schoolhouse. The hall was also where area kids could turn in the gopher claws for "bounty." It would be open Monday nights for this purpose in the summer months.

The hall was also where voting occurred.

Many townships began to flourish after World War II when the men and most boys came home. Tractors replaced horses, and combines became common as threshing machines were put out to pasture. Most farms now had

electricity, and many houses had telephones.

Threshing machines put out to pasture.

No one was divorced or worked on Sunday. Golf was something town people did, and the local cemeteries looked nice. Viking Township was ideal, and it was a great time to be alive.

Although telephones were becoming more common, not every family had one so township messages were mainly relayed three ways; kids delivering messages to neighboring farms, the mailman as he drove his route, and the township news column in the county paper written by a woman who didn't have kids at home anymore. In Viking Township, these positions were held, respectively, by Dougie Johnson, Earl on Rural Route One and Tillie Torkelson.

Eight-year-old Dougie was too young to do much field work so it fell to him to pass on messages to neighbors, and he loved it. Sometimes he would cut across the pasture or a field, sometimes he rode his bike on the road, but usually

he walked the road pulling his banged up red Flyer wagon. Wearing his Davy Crockett cap, he became a neighborhood spectacle who held the center of Viking Township together.

Dougie Johnson, the Carrier Pigeon for part of Viking Township

Except for silos and ants, most things in Dougie's world were four-and-a-half-feet tall. Viking Township had some hills, slopes, rivers and lakes, but for a four-and-a-half foot kid the surroundings were mainly four-and-a-half feet tall — cattails, Baltimore Orioles on fence posts and mailboxes. Little kids see things at their own level.

Dougie's Universe

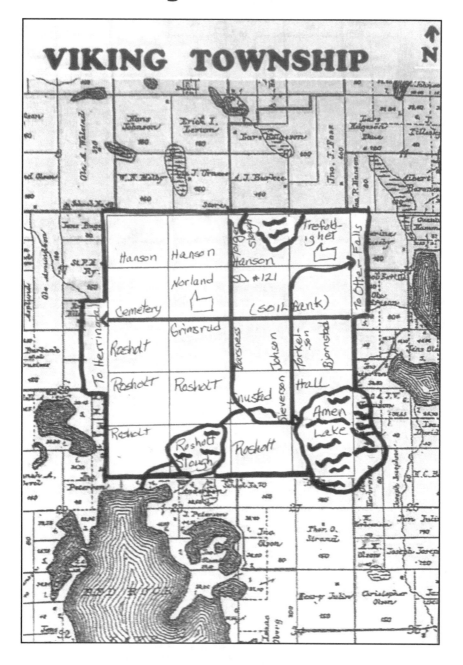

Dougie's Universe

The center of Dougie's universe held his parents, Art and Arlys Johnson, Grandma Tillie Torkelson and the closest neighbors — all Scandinavian-Americans.

There were two churches in his little universe. It seems that many who lived in the eastern part of his universe traveled west to church, and many in the west drove east to church. They would meet each other on the road, and give them the "steering wheel pointer-finger-wave." One didn't join the closest church, but went to the one their parents had attended.

❖ ❖

Art, Arlys and Dougie Johnson: Small-grain farmers and raised a variety of animals, herd of 18 Holsteins. Norwegians. *Trefoldighet* Lutheran.

Arlys, who had been a Dairy Princess at the Fish County Fair, was the only offspring of Tillie and Torsten Torkelson. She married Art Johnson, who had grown up north of Herringdal, in 1950 at *Trefoldighet* Lutheran in Viking Township. They started out helping Tillie and Torsten with the farming. A year later, their son, Dougie, was born.

A year after that, Torsten died unexpectedly from silo

asphyxiation, a silo gas poisoning caused by the natural fermentation of recently chopped corn silage. Torsten was only 52 years old, and had almost paid off the mortgage.

It was a very sad time for the people in Viking Township and Fish County. Torsten had been one of the most active 4-H leaders around, and had helped other chapters get started. He had also served on the Fish County Fair Board, and was treasurer at *Trefoldighet* Lutheran. In anticipation of the biggest event ever at *Trefoldighet,* church men showed up a day before the funeral and mowed the ditches with sickle mowers and a bush hog so the cars could park in the ditches. The mortuary brought extra men along to direct traffic and handle the crowd. Even Johnny Grimsrud, who rarely played in public, played his violin at the service.

In the weeks to come, Tillie adjusted to this loss better than Arlys did. Arlys kept thinking of the wonderful times she had with her father. She began to think more about Dougie and what kind of man he would become. She remembered things she hadn't thought about for years, like Dougie's first week of school in first grade.

Arlys had bought him some new school clothes he could grow into, and every morning she reminded him to brush his teeth and put on clean underwear. By Thursday of that week, Dougie complained that his new jeans were too tight. When Arlys asked him to show her, she noticed he had four pair of underwear on. Yes, he had put on clean underwear each day — but put

them on over the underwear from the days before.

Art and Arlys decided to buy most of her parent's land, but saved ten acres for Tillie. On those ten acres, they built a small house for her across the road and just east of the home place. She had room for a garage and several gardens, and was within walking distance from the homeplace.

In time, Dougie, unknowingly, started to follow in his grandfather's footsteps. Dougie became the glue that held the center of the township together.

(Lawrence) Butch, Evelyn, and Baby Larry Barsness: Beginning farmers, Norwegians, *Nordland* Lutheran

One morning, after he had fed the chickens, picked the eggs and put the table scraps into the dog dish, his mom asked eight-year-old Dougie to bring some magazines ("Readers' Digest," "Successful Farming" and "The Lutheran Standard") to Evelyn, the closest neighbor to the west.

Actually, Dougie's mom was a little concerned because

Evelyn was "due" any day, and no one had heard anything. Evelyn's husband, Butch, was sort of the gray sheep of the township, and Evelyn was the one who kept the "till death do us part" together. Butch boasted around the township that if Evelyn was going to pop out a boy, he was going to name him Manure, Manure Barsness, and call him Shit for short.

Dougie happily took off pulling his wagon with the three magazines tucked between some empty Ball jars he always hauled along for collecting bugs. Along the way he would load his wagon with treasures; pop bottles to redeem in town, and special rocks and stones perfect for his slingshot. Once in a while he even found lost hubcaps. His current goal in life was to have his own scrap iron business, DJ's Scrap Iron.

Dougie heard some odd sounds when he got to Evelyn's house, but he just rapped like he usually did and walked in. He didn't see her so he yelled, "Hi, It's Dougie. My mom sent me over with some stuff for you." He could hear some scary noises coming from upstairs. He panicked and yelled loudly, "Ya, where are you, then?" Evelyn yelled back, "Help, I'm in the bedroom. Please help me!"

Dougie threw the reading stuff down on the kitchen table and ran up the stairs. Evelyn was sitting up in bed, chewing on a washcloth, and wiggling and squirming like an angle worm that had been cut in half.

Dougie had heard a sound like that before in the barn, and he took off for home dumping the treasures out of the wagon. When he got to the main road he hopped in the wagon making the most of a downhill ride and steering with the handle. His mother heard him coming and ran to meet him. Dougie jumped up and down like he did when he had to go to the bathroom and couldn't hold it anymore, and said, "I have to go now! Right now! NO NO! I mean YOU have to go right now. Evelyn just keeps bellowing. I think she's calfing!"

Dougie's mom grabbed a bath towel and took off in the '55 Chevy heading for Evelyn's. Dougie, hot and confused, walked off behind the chicken coop where he had a secret fort. He plopped down and grabbed the jar that held his wood tick collection. Farm kids learn the facts of life early, but they generally apply only to animals. Dougie had seen and heard calves and pigs be born, but it had never occurred to him that people might go through something similar. He put some long grass in his mouth to chew on, and held the precious jar. He had a lot to think about.

Evelyn had grown up in Hatcher, the next county to the west of Fish County. She met Butch at Thursday night roller-skating in Everdale when she was a senior in high school. Butch had recently been discharged from the Navy, and had spent the past four years in the Pacific.

As soon as he could grow his hair out, Butch threw away his Butch Wax and grew a duck-tail, sleeking it back with Wildroot Cream Oil, and splashing his neck with Old Spice. Evelyn was smitten.

Butch brought home some spicy language from the Navy,

but Evelyn's parents liked him, and figured he must have some discipline because he had been honorably discharged. The night of the wedding, Butch carried Evelyn over the barn threshold, and every morning Butch got up first and percolated the coffee. Evelyn felt like Queen Elizabeth.

Butch made an offer on his uncle's 80-acre farm, and it was his! His land adjoined Johnson's to the east, and Mrs. Snustad's to the south. The land across the road to the north of Johnson's was owned by a city person, a nephew of Tolger Flessland, and was in the Soil Bank program. When the ten years in the Soil Bank were up, Butch was hoping to acquire it. To earn money for the purchase, he worked part-time for Harvey's Auctioneering.

Other than roller-skating, young Evelyn hadn't developed a lot of talents yet, but because she was married to Butch, she was getting very good at washing clothes. She was also conservation-minded. After every laundry day, she had Butch carry the galvanized tub of used rinse water out to the garden. Evelyn would dip the water on the plants.

Another talent she believed she had perfected was baking Funny Face Cookies. Ten years ago, she had received the <u>Let's Cook with Gail</u> cookbook for her birthday. She decided to make the first recipe in the book for her dad. The Funny Face Cookies she made were rather salty and had an odd texture, but like most Lutheran dads, he praised them. This odd compliment inspired Evelyn to make them weekly for the next eight years. If she didn't have cream of tartar, she used baking powder. She wasn't sure what a teaspoon of soda would do, so she left it out. Besides, where she lived people called it pop, not soda like called for in the recipe. They rarely had pop in their house. And, one teaspoon of vanilla looked rather cool as it swirled in the batter when she stirred it, so she often added more vanilla.

These cookies were also one of the first things she made for Butch. Like her father, Butch praised the cookies, so she kept making them. She would also bring them to church for "doings" and to parties. She dreamed about submitting them at the Fish County Fair and winning a ribbon.

Butch and her father had discovered that even their pigs couldn't really handle them, so the men buried them so Evelyn wouldn't see what they did with her Funny Face Cookies made with optional ingredients.

If Dougie's universe had a character, it was Butch. He was always telling stories, and it was hard to tell if he made them up or if they were true. One morning he told Dougie that it was so foggy, the chickens laid eggs on the puffs of fog. Another time Dougie noticed that Butch's hand was all scratched up. Shy Dougie asked him what happened. Butch, with his typical grin on his face, answered, "Oh, I vas yust shasing a fart trew a nail keg." Dougie didn't ask anymore, but sure thought about it on his walk home. Once when Larry was very little, Butch and Evelyn had brought the baby to a birthday party, and placed him on a bed with all the visitors' coats. They forgot to take the baby home. Butch taught Dougie about birds and cats. He called nuthatches the "hind-end-up-a-tree bird." He said if cats ate grass, it was going to rain. Butch seemed like a rough guy, but he had a soft side. Dougie noticed he always squirted milk to the kittens when he was milking. If a cow stepped on a kitten or if a cat proudly dragged home a bird or the dog dragged home a rabbit, Butch always gave the deceased animals a somewhat proper burial. Whenever someone left the Barsnesses, Butch would say, "You behave now, and if you can't behave, come over." In spite of his random crudeness, people in the area did like Butch.

Perhaps Butch's best trick occurred when the county decided it had to place a bigger culvert between Barsnesses and Rosholts to the southwest. Butch was opposed to it because it would take some of his pasture land. He went to the Fish County Board meeting to oppose it, but the motion to install it passed. The morning they began working on it, Butch was out there with his spicy language. Finally, the sheriff was called. As the sheriff was handcuffing Butch and moving him toward the sheriff's car, Butch just happened to (deliberately) slip on some fresh cow pies. He rolled several times, and the sheriff had to put a smelly, wet trouble-maker in the sheriff's car. Old Spice didn't do anything for Butch or the car that day.

Johnny, Hazel, and Gloria Jean Grimsrud:
Blacksmith and Saw-sharpening, Small Farmers, Piano Teacher, Norwegians, *Nordland* Lutheran.

Across the North-South road to the west of the Barsness place was where the Grimsruds lived. Some days Dougie might be asked to go to the Grimsruds, crossing the intersection, to borrow some tools for his dad. Johnny had a whole garage full of tools. He did blacksmithing and saw-sharpening for the neighborhood, and for people miles around.

If Dougie timed it right, Johnny would be in the house

having his forenoon lunch, and Johnny's Mrs. would welcome Dougie and tell him to come in. He would be given a chair and offered some donuts

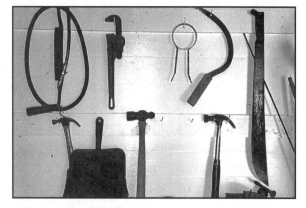

and Watkins nectar. Every time Hazel gave him a doughnut she would say, "Now don't eat the hole." The first few times Dougie ate all around the hole, but he soon caught on to her joke.

Across the road to the north of Grimsrud's was the *Nordland* Lutheran Church where Hazel was the organist. She was also the piano teacher in

38

that part of Viking Township, and felt she was called by God to make sure *Nordland* Lutheran never ran out of pianists and organists. Books in the <u>John Thompson's Modern Course for the Piano</u> series were passed among her students as one student would quit lessons and another started. Before he left to go to the garage with Johnny for tools, Hazel would urge Dougie to consider taking piano lessons. After all, Grieg and Bach were men.

Nordland Lutheran had a special Rite of Passage for some piano students. Whenever one of Hazel's students made it through "Bill Grogan's Goat" (with F#) in <u>John Thompson Book Two</u>, Hazel would notify the student's parents who would then notify aunts and uncles and Baptism sponsors that the following Sunday that student would be playing something special. Like clockwork, regardless of where they were in the church year, the lucky student would be asked to play the right hand for "Nearer, My God to Thee" (with F#), the congregation would sing, and Hazel would pound out the left-hand part. The student hated it and the congregation was in pain, but Mrs. Grimsrud loved it and played her part with some jazzy intervals. She felt great because she believed she was now a bit closer to God's mission for her — to provide future pianists and organists for *Nordland*.

When Gloria Jean wasn't practicing piano, she liked to be on the field with her dad. She always brought him lunch; a fresh "termos" of coffee, two sandwiches wrapped in waxed paper or in the lining from a cereal box, and a bar. Hazel made sure there was enough lunch for Gloria

Jean too, and Gloria Jean and her dad would sit in the shade of the large tractor wheel. After lunch, Johnny would take Gloria Jean for a round on the field. She would sit on the toolbox or the big fender, depending upon the tractor.

Another of Gloria Jean's jobs was to get the cows home at milking time. She had named each one and called them by name as well as using the standard, "Come boss. Come boss." If it was supper time and her dad was still on the field, she would stand on the porch and wave a white dishtowel and holler, "Yoo-hoo. Supper time."

The two, Gloria Jean and her dad, made special plans and a special lunch when he was plowing. They knew the seagulls would be diving into the fresh dirt,

and that was the time when Gloria Jean would look for arrowheads. She usually found some, and hoped that one year these rocks could become a special 4-H project.

On summer evenings, when there was little wind, neighbors could hear Johnny — who was sitting on his porch — playing his violin. Dougie's universe was a peaceful place to live.

Nordland Lutheran Church and Cemetery: Congregation organized by Norwegians from middle Norway in 1888.Built in 1889—1890. Originally the Norwegian Synod, but since 1917 The Norwegian Lutheran Church of America. Current pastor: Rev. A.l. Torstenson

This was located on the corner north of Grimsruds, west of the Soil-Banked land, kitty-corner to Barsnesses and south of Hansons.

❖ ❖

The Hansons: Siblings Floyd, Lloyd, Tillman and Bertha: Animal and Small Grain Farmers, Hired Man and Housekeeper. Norwegians. *Trefoldighet* Lutheran Church.

Just to the north of *Nordland* Lutheran was the Hanson farm. Larger and more established than Barsnesses or Grimsruds, the Hanson parents had left 40 acres to each of their children: twins Floyd and Lloyd, Tillman and Bertha. Tillman really had no interest in owning land, but liked to work with animals and to help where he could. He sold his 40 acres to his two brothers, and went to work a mile south for the Rosholts as a hired hand. He would stay at the Rosholts, but went home for holidays and when he needed clothes washed. That wasn't very often.

Dougie usually biked to the Hansons because of the distance, but if he walked, he took his imaginary friend, Jimmy, along. They talked about many things from rocks to school to peanut butter sandwiches.

Floyd and Lloyd were almost always together and spent their lives working. They raised wheat, oats, barley, corn and their sister's flax. They talked about planting soybeans the next year. They had 20 Herefords and wanted to expand the herd. They had pigs and chickens a few sheep. Other than farming, they went to church, *Lutefisk* suppers, to town for parts and on the Fourth of July.

The twins had an odd characteristic. They would not switch to Daylight Saving Time (DST) once it became a standard procedure. Their father had told them what happened when they switched to DST during World War II, and the twins didn't want to risk this. Their dad said that the cows couldn't adjust, and the cows couldn't wait, and he had lost probably $80 in seven months of DST.

Milk production had gone way down. Almost every Sunday during those months, the Hansons had been late for church services, and arrived smelling barn.

Bertha, who was the oldest and had to quit school after eight grades to stay home and take care of her mother and brothers, hired the twins to work her 40 acres. Every year she had them plant flax on her acreage. She knew about the benefits of crop rotation, but just adored the color periwinkle. The flax flowers didn't last that long, but they brought her such joy while they did. Bertha could use joy.

In addition to 40 acres of periwinkle, one other thing that brought Bertha joy was making flatbread, i.e., *flatbrød*. She whistled while she rolled it out, and everyone agreed she did make wonderful flatbread. She was always asked to bring it to church events. It contained intricate designs unlike those from fork tines. It was a local mystery, but one night when Tillman was a little tipsy at *Trefoldighet's Lutefisk* Supper, he mentioned how the designs got there. Bertha, who raised chickens and could chop their heads off with one whack, also had a pet chicken she kept in the house. She had had this pet, Elvira, for six years, and when Bertha whistled making flatbread, the chicken had "free range." Elvira danced on the table when Bertha was near, and especially when Bertha whistled. A variation of the Chicken Dance was apparently allowed in some Lutheran homes. Tillman, who had saved some money after he cut back on alcohol, bought Bertha and Elvira a periwinkle-colored bedspread that year for Christmas.

Once school consolidation had been completed in the early '50s, the twins rented the school land across the road around the old #121 school building. They fenced it in, and used it as a cow pasture. Once in a while the cows would get out, even on Sunday mornings, creating chaos at *Nordland* Lutheran, especially for the ushers. Sometimes the cows ran to both *Nordland* and *Trefoldighet* Churches. They were obviously Lutheran cows.

Bertha was also the main butcherer for chickens in the township, and had perfected the art of shearing sheep.

❖ ❖

The Rosholts: Rollef(d.) and Halvilde(d.) and Ralph. Ralph and Olga and Russell. Russell and Shirley and Rodney and Roger. Roger and Carol and Richard. Norwegians. *Trefoldighet* Lutheran.

South of Grimsruds was the biggest and oldest farm in Dougie's universe, the Rosholt Farm. Rollef and Halvilde homesteaded there in 1861 clearing some of the land near Rosholt slough and building the first house and barn on the property. Their son, Ralph, eventually married Olga and they begat Russell. Russell married Shirley, and they begat Rodney and Roger who were twins and friends of Dougie.

The twins and Dougie would holler through the culvert that ran under the road by Mrs. Snustad's. One spring morning when the water was really running, Dougie had talked his dad into sawing a 1" X 4" board into a boat, and the boys would "sail" this through the culvert. It worked great sailing it one direction, but didn't go too well against the current. They would just take the boat and run across the road with it, and sail it again. Sometimes, they just had distance-peeing contests or climbed trees. Once in a while they would put tin cans on fence posts and practice shooting with their BB guns. They couldn't wait until they were older and could shoot swallows and sparrows in the hay barn.

Russell had been the first person in that area to have a car radio and he often said that's how he won Shirley over. He could pick up two AM regional stations. One played 85 percent milking music, and he also had the barn radio set to that station. That station also played the noon stock report, and some local and world news including Gabriel Heatter and Walter Winchell. The other station played a variety of music and that is what he usually played in the car.

Shirley took care of the house with Olga, but was usually found in the car or pick-up driving to area towns for parts. The Rosholts had a big farm with lots of machinery to break down. In time, she became known as the Parts Runner, and would sometimes pickup parts her neighbors needed. She knew she would be Parts Runner for many years because when the twins were old enough to drive, they would be needed in the fields or barn. Thank heavens Russell only bought vehicles with a radio.

The Widow Snustad: Widow and gardener. Norwegian. *Trefoldighet* Lutheran.

Dougie's least favorite place to go would be to Widow Snustad's who lived across from Rosholt's farm just south of Barsnesses. She rented out her land to Rosholts, and she liked to talk and would ask questions about the neighborhood, school, the minister, and always said how dry things were.

Dougie only went to her house to invite her to some township event or to bring her bad news. Each time Dougie got there, she would remind him to "Wipe your feet." The widow's replies to Dougie's news were always the same. She couldn't possibly go to anything because she didn't have a nice dress to wear or her gout and corns were acting up or her feet would be too swollen to get shoes on. Her bunions were just awful these days. She didn't want to drive anywhere because she was saving her car to get to church services. She got so concerned about cars going too fast on the curve between her farm and Rosholts that she had the county install a special sign there.

When there was bad news to deliver, Dougie sat through the same, sad monologue; death was awful, the hurt never left the survivors, her Sven had been a wonderful man and "they don't make them like him any more," his funeral service was so big and the lunch was so good, and here she is now – with her gout and swollen feet – left to do all the work.

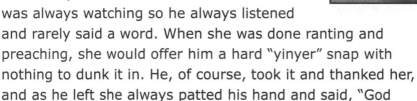

Dougie knew the speech by heart, but he was a patient Lutheran who knew God was always watching so he always listened and rarely said a word. When she was done ranting and preaching, she would offer him a hard "yinyer" snap with nothing to dunk it in. He, of course, took it and thanked her, and as he left she always patted his hand and said, "God bless you." Then she yelled, "Don't slam the screen door."

Sometimes Dougie hauled her squash from the garden to her porch in his wagon. One year she had a lot of squash so she asked him to bring some to each of the neighbors. Another time a man's boot had shown up on the widow's porch. She figured Barsness's dog had delivered it, and she asked Dougie to put it in his wagon and find the owner. She didn't need a man's boot on her porch. What if the minister came to visit?

One day when she was particularly lonesome, she told Dougie that this past winter she had taken time to put her napkin collection into scrapbooks, and it took three albums. "Did he want to see them?" Dougie, who rarely uttered a word when he was with her, simply said, "I have to get home to help with the milking." That was a lie, and Dougie knew it. The whole way home he prayed for forgiveness, and when he made it home he went straight to the barn and asked his parents, "Can I please help?"

Tillie Torkelson: Widow, Columnist and Grandmother. Norwegian. *Trefoldighet* Lutheran.

Northeast of the Widow Snustad's place and directly east of Johnsons was where Tillie Torkelson lived. She had sold most of her land to Dougie's dad and mom, Art and Arlys. Tillie was lonesome after her only child, Arlys, got married, so to occupy her time, she wrote the Viking Township News for the "Fish County Weekly" and never missed the Wednesday deadline.

As a result of this job she knew perhaps more about the people living there than anyone else in Viking. She also knew things that she considered not fit to print, and sometimes wished she had amnesia because it was hard to see some of those people in church.

Grandma Tillie often asked Dougie to find out if any neighbors had any news for her column. Sometimes the oral messages became like a game of Crazy Telephone. The wrong person died, another wrong person was "PG," and a brother was labeled as having one of his brothers' cancer. Many of these important — but erroneous — messages were then printed in the township column in the "Fish County Weekly," and occasionally congregations prayed for the wrong person.

Tillie had a sister, Tekla, who lived in Herringdal. Whenever Tillie had errands in town, she selected Herringdal over Otter Falls so Tekla could accompany her shopping. They were best friends. Both of them had grandchildren about the same age, Dougie and Bonnie, and the grandmas tried to get the kids together once a month. Usually Tekla and Bonnie would drive from Otter Falls to Tillie's where Tillie would fix Dougie's "favorite meal in the whole wide world." The four of them sat down to ring baloney, canned pork and beans, watermelon pickles, and dessert that Bonnie and Tekla had made.

After noon dinner, the sisters would do dishes while Dougie and Bonnie played outside. Sometimes they played anti-I-over at the garage, sometimes they each hopped on an end of Tillie's huge propane tank and "rode horsey." Other times they played leapfrog or built a tent putting a blanket over the clothesline. They would sit in the tent and read until their grandmas brought them lunch.

Once Bonnie taught Dougie to make dolls out of hollyhocks, and he taught her to make farting sounds by placing a hand in the opposite armpit. Bonnie would hold dandelions under Dougie's chin to see if he liked butter. When they had been seven-years-old and had loose teeth, they would put a string around the tooth and tie the other end to a doorknob, and open and shut the door trying to get the tooth out. Eventually, the grandmas had enough of the door-slamming. Sometimes they had a playhouse under some trees. Dougie called it a fort. Bonnie called it a playhouse. They made rugs using the big leaves of Burdock plants and used the poisonous stems for rhubarb. They had cattails for hotdogs, Caragana pods for peas, stones for potatoes and little green pinecones and fake dill for pickles. They would decorate the tree stump table with field mustard for a bouquet. If it was raining, they played school in Tillie's house.

Their favorite thing to do, however, was to simply lie on the grass and look at the clouds. They saw clowns, mountain ranges, angels, dragons, dinosaurs, fairies and elephants. When that got old, or the clouds were gone, they would take Dougie's wagon and go on the main road looking for treasures in the ditches. Once they found a trailer hitch, and Dougie knew that would be added to his growing pile which would become part of DJ's Scrap Iron someday. Their favorite finds, though, were discarded glass pop bottles. They would redeem these in town and split the proceeds for Lifesavers, bubble gum and marshmallow circus peanuts. Once they bought candy cigarettes. They didn't taste so great, and left white marks on their lips. Tillie and Tekla were a little upset about this, but when the kids were out of earshot, Tillie and Tekla got the giggles like some teenagers in church. They couldn't stop laughing.

In the winter, they would build snowmen or go sliding using old "fender skirts" and even fenders for sleds.

Someday Dougie was going to ask Grandma Tillie if he could have them for his scrap pile.

Once Bonnie brought doll clothes along, and the two kids had a great time dressing up Tillie's cats and chickens.

Grandma Tillie told the kids that once the crops were planted and before haying started, she would see if Art could put two rubber tire swings in her boxelder tree. It seems she always kept the kids anticipating something new.

These monthly visits of Dougie and Tillie and Bonnie and Tekla would always be given space in Tillie's column in Viking Township News in the "Fish County Weekly."

❖ ❖

Trefoldighet Lutheran Church and Cemetery: Congregation organized by Norwegians from southern Norway, mainly Haugeans, in 1866. Built in 1876—1879. Originally the Hauge Synod, but since 1917 The Norwegian Lutheran Church of America. Current pastor: Rev. Lars Kjeldstad.

❖ ❖

The Bjornstads: Lawrence and Edna and nine children. Struggling farmers. Norwegian. *Nordland* Lutheran.

Lawrence and Edna (Stordahl) Bjornstad and their truckload of kids lived just to the east of Tille Torkelson. If Tille was ever short on news, she knew she would come by some visiting the Bjornstads. There was always something going on there with that brood.

Once when Tillie went there, Edna was cleaning out the cistern. The youngest two kids were tied up to the clothesline so they wouldn't fall in the cistern, and the oldest four were helping haul and dump pails of the dirty water on the garden. When that job was done, Edna was planning to make soap.

The three very oldest children were helping Lawrence pick rocks and mustard on the south 20. By now those kids were old enough to take turns driving the Allis or loading rocks onto the stone-boat. Another time Tillie was there, Lawrence came driving the pickup home from the field. There were kids in the cab, kids in the back, and more kids hanging on to the sides and standing on the running boards.

Often there were pigs in the garden or the cows would be running loose. When they weren't working in the field, Lawrence and the older boys were dehorning cattle or castrating pigs. Even with all the available help, the Bjornstads' work never seemed to be done.

The Bjornstads had grabbed Tillie's heart, but there was little she could do. If there was food left over from an event at *Trefoldighet* Lutheran, the kitchen workers would load Tillie up with it knowing where the food would end up. Tillie would stop by Bjornstads' on her way home from church and tell them that she couldn't possibly eat all that. Would they like some? She couldn't let it go to waste. The older boys almost attacked her, but they all said thank you. Once, just for fun, Tillie stopped there with a big watermelon from town. She said she hadn't seen a seed-spitting contest for years. Would they comply? She'd even give fifty cents to the one who spit the farthest. Mom and dad and Tillie even took part in the spitting contest. The oldest boy, of course, won. When it was time for Tillie to leave, two of the little girls told her they had never had so much fun.

At this time, in the mid-'50s, "welfare" cases were still handled by the Fish County Sheriff's Office. Each year the sheriff made sure every poor family with children had a box of food delivered. It wasn't tin-canned food like today, but canned goods from area gardens. That year Tillie and her sister, Tekla, went to the sheriff's department in November to make a proposal. These sisters wanted to take care of the box for the Bjornstads. Tillie and Tekla provided jars of food that they had canned, and some jellies and loaves of bread from Arlys. They got an embroidered tablecloth made by Selma Sieverson, and five dollars from both Anna Sieverson and the Widow Snustad. Tillie and Tekla went shopping. They bought five tablets, five pencils, and four coloring books and four boxes of color crayons for the kids, and a new white handkerchief and two red field ones for Lawrence. They wrapped these up along with the tablecloth for Edna, and put them in the food box. Tekla had lined up four neighbors in Otter Falls to donate different kinds of Christmas cookies. Tillie wrote out nine Christmas cards for the kids. They put the ten dollars they had collected in a Christmas card in the box addressed to Lawrence and Edna. Then Tekla brought it to the sheriff's department to be delivered with the other "welfare" boxes. The Rosholts brought them two quarts of whole cream so the Bjornstads could have *rømmegrøt* for Christmas. That year the Bjornstads believed in both Jesus and Santa Claus.

With so many children, salesmen just assumed Bjornstads were Catholics. Not so. Their children made up 75 percent of the Sunday School children at *Nordland* Lutheran, and they rarely missed a Sunday.

There were so many Stordahls in Fish County that they decided to start their own family cemetery. Edna Stordahl, who was married to Lawrence Bjornstad, decided she was going to be buried by her man in the Nordland Lutheran Cemetery. Her decision caused such a big uproar in the Stordahl Family that some of them showed their disapproval by skipping the funeral. Most of them came for the lunch, though.

Sieverson "Girls": Selma and Anna. Spinsters. Peony Grower and poet. Seamstress and handiwork. Norwegians. *Nordland* Lutheran.

Directly south of Johnsons and to the southeast of the Widow Snustad's place was where Selma and Anna Sieverson, two spinster sisters, lived. Although they were both over 65 years old, everyone referred to them as the Sieverson Girls!

They lived on the family farm, but only used the house and outhouse. They rented out the land and barn to Rosholts. Russell Rosholt once suggested they should invest in indoor plumbing. Selma snapped back, "If God wanted toilets in the house he would have put them there." Another time Russell went to the girls' place to haul some bales back to the Rosholt farm. He heard a loud bang and noticed that Anna had opened a screen-less window over the sink and was shooting a squirrel that was clawing in the flower garden. No one and nothing messed with her peonies. She furnished *Nordland* with peonies when she could. Anna also wrote poetry and liked to read her poems for Ladies' Aid meetings. She became known as the Peony and Poetry Girl.

Selma had been a dressmaker in Otter Falls, and now she did occasional tailoring. She mostly did handiwork: knitting, crocheting, *Klostersøm, Hardangersøm* and needlepoint. She had made most of the altar cloths at *Nordland*. Selma didn't like conflict. Anna said that Selma was usually mending clothes or mending fences. When Anna's sense of humor came through, she would say, "I keep people in stitches."

They subscribed to the "Decorah *Posten*," and would squabble over who got to read the "Ola *og* Per" cartoon first. One year for Christmas, Anna had made a scrapbook for Selma filled with these cartoons, and they were even funnier the second time through them.

To the east of their farm was the Viking Township Hall and Amen Lake where kids swam, and adults fished and picnicked. Watching the comings and goings at both places kept the Sieverson Girls busy.

Amen Lake

This was a beautiful, small lake surrounded by trees that turned lovely colors in the Fall. The Viking Township Hall was just off the main road, and led to the road by the lake. The shoreline wasn't mown, but the water was basically without weeds.

In the Spring, churches used the property for Sunday School year-end picnics, and sometimes *Trefoldighet* and *Nordland* Congregations would have a joint picnic. Also, it was a great fishing lake used from May through ice-over, and sometimes even then for ice-fishing, which was just getting popular.

But, it was in the summer that Amen Lake came to life. On hot summer days, swimming was a township-wide event, especially for those nearest this lake. Even the Finns from the southeastern part of the township came. People were encouraging the Viking Victory 4-H Club to take on a community project of building a raft. Ten years earlier, the club had built a short dock.

Women and children would head to the lake in the late afternoon. The men would come later when they were done on the field and after the milking. By then the women and children had gone home.

Unbeknownst to most, at 9:00 p.m. or so, the lake belonged to the men. (Tillie, of course, knew but told no one, not even Tekla.) The men brought their homemade soap and towels to the lake, took their swimming trunks off and ran in. It was a great way to get rid of the field dirt, and in August, the only way to ease "barley itch." It isn't known when this skinny-dipping, "Cleanliness is next to Godliness" tradition began, but it became more popular each year. Little did the men know that the Sieverson "Girls," the spinster sisters, had a pair of binoculars.

We are all better people because of folks like those in Viking Township, and especially Dougie."...and a little child shall lead them." (Is.11:6) Amen!

Amen Lake

Part II
Surviving on Sweat, Storms and Struggles

We had Drifts as High as the Brooder House

and as high as the barn

and as high as the house

To this day, Norwegian Lutherans love to talk about the weather. The more challenging the weather, the more excited they get. It's in their DNA, and weather is the only thing that gets them talking out loud in public to complete strangers.

When preparing for changing weather, we knew what we needed to do and when and how to "weather the weather." When the geese were honking and flying south in the fall, we got out the tarpaper and hay bales and banked the house. We lined up "town homes" for rural school kids to stay at when the snow was coming down so hard and fast that we knew we would have drifts as high as the brooder house.

When the rivers overflowed their banks and threatened to

flood the farm, we knew how to quickly move people, cattle, and canned gooseberries out of harm's way. We sharpened the ice picks, axes and shovels to break up the ice jams that were clogging the culverts and preventing the runoff from going where God intended it to go. In the summer, we all crunched into the storm cellars when we saw dark clouds and funnels in the sky, and hail pelting our crops.

We called climate change "weather," and we knew it was changing when we felt it, saw it and heard it. There was no such thing as breaking news to warn us of bad weather. If a siren went off, it was to remind us that it was time to eat noon dinner, not necessarily to take cover in the storm cellar or to "duck and cover" under our school desks.

People in Dougie's Universe joked that they had their own weather service. Anna Sieverson's bones knew 12 hours ahead of a thunderstorm, and her sister, Selma's, joints could predict 24 hours ahead of high humidity. Two days before the barometric pressure dropped and a front was coming through, Tillie Torkelson knew the weather was changing because she felt it in her bones. People on Dougie's route would ask him what Anna, Selma and Tillie were predicting.

Orlin Bjerke could verify the wind direction by spitting on

his finger. When Orlin was driving his wife, Hilda, and Tillie Torkelson home from Ladies Aid, they didn't need anyone to tell them that it was too windy back there, then. They had to roll up the backseat car windows and secure their breeze bonnets because of all the dust and cottonwood tree fluff that was whirling and swirling around inside the car.

Climate change was verified by TV weathermen, who weren't called fancy names like meteorologists. Dewey Bergquist[1], the Fargo WDAY weatherman, was pretty good at letting his audiences know when a corker was coming out of the west.

We also trusted our mercury barometers and rain gauges to prove what we felt, saw and heard.

The Farmer's Almanac, a book that everybody bought at the local drug store and read in January when there wasn't any field work to do, was full of predictions that most people believed were nothing more than guesses.

---

[1]Dewey Bergquist used humor to get his point across. "Watch out for blowing and drifting billboards." Dewey had Swedish roots, and it was rare for a Swede to have a sense of humor. He was one of the first guests on Verna Newell's "Party Line" television show, and was really comfortable bantering back and forth with her.

When I was Three I Ate Mud and Chewed Wheat

When we were kids, we yanked carrots and potatoes out of the ground and ate them raw along with the mud that clung to them. We made our own gum by chewing wheat kernels from wheat heads, and sucked the nectar out of honeysuckles. We ate the brown spots on bananas, and worm holes on apples if they weren't too big. We begged for "boughten" penny candy and ice cream cones, and hoped the county extension people would someday realize they should be included in The Basic Seven food groups.

Our food came from the barn, the lakes, the land, the sky and woods – except for lutefisk, herring, and sardines which came from Norway. Our local grocer provided a few essentials like sugar, salt, flour, coffee, mild spices, baking supplies, nuts and lugs of fruit like Freestone or cling peaches that couldn't be grown in our area. We bought our vanilla and nectar from the Watkins man.

In the summer, we picked, snipped, cleaned, canned and froze the produce we grew, and skinned, filleted and froze the fish we caught. In the fall, we picked potatoes, hunted and butchered animals. Like squirrels, we stocked up for the long winter months, and sometimes we even shot them before they had collected all the acorns they were gathering to store.

We abided by the rule, waste not, want not, and when we butchered we preserved the "whole hog." We made head cheese out of the head innards and ham, pork chops and roast out of the body insides. We pickled the pigs' feet, and rendered the fat for lard, i.e., Norwegian Lutheran olive oil. Leftover roast was saved to be used for pork sandwiches, and if there was still some more roast left, it was ground up to be made into hash.

Meals at home were served five to six times a day. They included breakfast, lunch, dinner, lunch, and supper. Sometimes we ate lunch after supper if company was visiting. Our main meals were hardy, and at the minimum included meat, potatoes, vegetables and bread. We never had snacks, but we had lunches, and they would include sandwiches, bars, coffee or nectar. Fast food was cream on bread, sometimes topped off with Karo syrup or chokecherry jelly.

We drank water, coffee and nectar. Coffee was the king of all beverages. We didn't drink tea because we were told that tea was for sick people, wimps, Episcopalians and town women who thought they were from Hollywood. Nectar was for kids, and served when the weather was hot, at home picnics and at church functions. Beer and hard liquor were drunk by Catholics out in the open, and some Lutherans drank it when nobody could see them.

We ate white food on a white plate in a white house. Most foods that we cooked or baked contained the basic white ingredients of flour, sugar, lard, cream and salt. If our food wasn't white, we turned it white. We took potatoes, peas, salmon and chipped beef and we creamed them and we turned them white. We creamed our corn and put white crackers all over the top, and we dumped cream into coffee and turned it white. We plastered large, white marshmallows all over the top of brightly-colored, orange squash.

We didn't eat much in the line of salads except for glorified rice, and Jell-O which was covered with whipped cream. The Germans ate coleslaw and sauerkraut, and all of us ate a little leaf lettuce that we called rabbit food.

Food served at church revolved around The Basic Six. They were hotdishes, open-face sandwiches, Jell-0, bars or cake, pickles and egg coffee. The only exception was the *Lutefisk* Supper where all stops were pulled out and all sorts of things were served.

As time marched on, different ideas and food began to creep into our kitchens and vocabularies. In 1954, when Gail Palmby, Clarence's daughter, advertised her cookbook, Let's Cook with Gail, in "The Farmer" magazine, it became an instant bestseller in Fish and Hatcher Counties. Girls started to make Funny Face cookies, and the cookies became the impetus that started the craze of decorating food to make it look appetizing and appealing. Women started taking classes on how to decorate cakes with frosting roses, and even some town women who spoiled their kids started making them snacks called Bumps on a Log, which was celery filled with peanut butter and decorated with raisins.

Foreign recipes started to creep into our vocabulary and cookbooks. Church cookbooks started to print recipes submitted by missionaries for Chicken Chow Mein. Before that time, the only foreign recipes we used came from the old country, but we didn't consider them foreign or put them in a special section in our church cookbooks.

To top it all off, a company called Chef Boyardee started promoting and selling boxes of pepperoni pizza. Fish County people called it pizza pie, and it became a hit with the youth of the area. The yellow-colored box contained dough, tomato sauce, parmesan cheese, and a spice called oregano that we had never heard of before in our life. The pizza pie was topped with a meat called pepperoni which looked like miniature summer sausage disks. Pizza pie became as popular as hotdish, except with Norwegian men who thought it was "too tomatoey."

Norwegian Lutheran Normal, Everyday, Standard Recipes

Ingredients for three basic normal hotdishes:

(1) Elbow macaroni, hamburger, tomato soup, corn and salt/pepper (2) Egg noodles, cut-up white chicken meat, cream of chicken soup, pale canned peas and salt/pepper (3) White rice, tuna fish, celery, cream of celery soup and salt/pepper.

Directions:

Brown the meat, but not tuna meat, of course, and boil the noodles or rice. The amount of ingredients to use depends upon the number of people to be served, so a person just has to gauge it. Mix it all up in no special order, and bake at 350 degrees for whatever amount of time it takes to get done.

Once when Helga Hanson brought a hamburger and potato hotdish to Ladies Aid, she hadn't baked it long enough and the potatoes were hard. When persnickety

Esther Mae Skogen tried to cut the potato, it flew off her plate and landed in the late Mrs. A.K. Olson's lap. Everyone saw it, didn't say anything, but thought it was about time. That woman was always acting like she was perfect, and was continuously criticizing everyone's kids.

Sandwiches

Ingredients and Directions all in one:

Sandwiches that were made at home consisted of a full bun or two slices of bread that were filled with summer sausage or some other cold meat. They were served to the men in the fields, in school lunch pails and for midday lunch breaks. Sandwiches that were served at church funerals were commonly known as "dead spreads," and were open-face. The three kinds of sandwiches that were served at Lutheran churches were:(1) ground-up ham or spam, homemade mayonnaise that was combined with pickle juice or relish, and served on white bread, (2) chopped-up, hard-boiled eggs that were mixed with pickle juice, chopped onions, homemade mayonnaise, salt and pepper, and served on wheat bread, and (3) Cheese Whiz spread on diagonally-cut buttered rye bread, and decorated with olive/pimento slices.

Jell-O

Ingredients for different types of Jell-0:
Jell-O from a box
Water
One banana, a can of fruit cocktail or pineapple
Celery
Whipping cream
Mayonnaise
Directions
They're on the Jell-O box.
The three basic recipes were: Red Jell-0 set with one

sliced banana and whipped cream added on top for company, Lime green Jell-O set with a can of pineapple and celery and covered with mayonnaise, Lemon Jell-O set with a can of fruit cocktail and no topping.

Note: *Jell-O was always served in the green-colored Pyrex nesting bowls that everyone received as a wedding gift.*

Cakes and Bars

Ingredients:

Favorite cakes were white, chocolate, marble and spice. Favorite bars were brownies, lemon and date. The basic ingredients for both cakes and bars are: flour, sugar, eggs, butter, baking powder and salt for cakes and bars, but cut out the baking powder for bars. Depending upon the cake or bar recipes, other ingredients such as chocolate, spices, dates and lemons would be added.

Directions:

Cream the butter and sugar, beat in the eggs, add the flour, the rest of the dry stuff and any other ingredients that are needed. Bake in a 9" x 13" pan at 350 degrees until done. Frost the cakes, and roll the bars in powdered sugar – but not the date bars.

Pickles

Ingredients:

Everyone canned and served seven basic types of pickles: dill, watermelon, chunky, sweet, beet, refrigerator and crab apple. Depending upon the type of pickle you were canning, you would need cucumbers, dill, watermelon rinds, crab apples or beets.

Directions:

Look for directions for making pickles in any church cookbook. For some of them, you might need a pressure cooker to get the job done.

Egg Coffee

Ingredients:

7 cups water

1 egg

2 tablespoons water

1/3 cup regular-grind coffee

Directions: - Bring seven cups of water to boiling in a white, enameled coffee pot. Remember an enameled coffee pot doesn't whistle like a tea kettle, so you have to watch what you are doing. Meanwhile, in a small bowl, beat the egg and two tablespoons of water with a fork. Stir the coffee into this mixture. When the water boils, add the coffee/egg mixture to the water and boil for seven minutes. Remove the pot from the heat and add ½ cup of cold water to settle the grounds.

Train up a child in the way
they should go . . .

. . . and when he is old, he will not depart from it.

(Proverbs 22:6)

Training in the Home

Training up a child was basically the responsibility of mothers, pastors and school teachers. Additional training came from dads, Sunday School teachers, piano instructors, 4-H leaders and older siblings. It did take a village to keep everyone in line!

Lullaby and Good Night

Training started immediately after a child was born, and within three weeks of their birth most kids were put on a schedule, feed solid food and expected to sleep through the night. If they didn't, they cried it out. When Dougie Johnson was old enough to recite "Now I lay me down to sleep . . ." and his mom had put him in his cowboy flannel pajamas for the night, he knew he didn't have an option to postpone his bedtime by trying to negotiate an extra glass of water.

Potty-training started as soon as a kid could sit without tipping over or being propped up. At about six to seven months, most kids were periodically plopped down on a wooden potty chair and were expected to sit there until they were able to tinkle in the metal cup that was attached to the chair. The tray was used for confinement, and not as a place to put Cherrios or little toys.

The goal was to get a child trained as soon as possible. If there were two kids born in a family within eight months of each other, rest assured, there was only one in a safety-pinned cloth diaper covered by rubber pants. In the '40s and

'50s there was no such thing as a size five disposable diaper.

When the "Dougie Johnsons of the township" were about three-years-old and playing by themselves outside, they used ditches, trees and the backside of buildings as a bathroom. When the urge hit, they would often find targets to aim at while peeing – like the middle of a tire, a puddle or anything handy. If they had an accident, even three-year-olds knew enough to face the wind so it would dry. Little girls would use the outhouse, and sometimes would have to hold on tight so they wouldn't fall in or off the "throne." Farm families also kept a #2 can underneath the sink for little boys to use when they didn't have time to make it up the stairs to the bathroom.

Think of all the Starving Kids in China

We ate all our meals at the table and not on TV trays in front of the couch or standing up while hanging over a counter. Everyone had a specific place to sit, and the only time we ate in our bedrooms was when we were quarantined because we had come down with something that was catchy. We started out our meal by saying grace – "Come Lord Jesus." Some families also had devotions before they ate.

We knew we had to eat what was served and clean up our plates, and if we didn't, we went hungry. If we didn't like the food or we sulked at being served liver, we were reprimanded and told to think of all the starving kids in China. During mealtime, we weren't expected to converse about how our day was going, but we knew we had to say please, as in "please pass the potatoes," and "thank you" after we ate. The girls knew enough to not even try to weasel their way out of doing dishes, and the boys were given instructions about the work around the farm that they were expected to do.

Social Training

Our parents did not cater to our whims or consider us as their friend. Basically, we were taught to think before we acted, behave, sit up straight, act decent, work hard and clean up our bodies and souls. If we were sick, we learned from observation that we would live and it would heal. We were expected to show respect for older people, teachers, leaders, pastors and anybody else who was in control. We were expected to pitch in and help anyone who needed it.

We were taught not to swear, let funny noises come out of our bodies, touch people we didn't know, kiss casual acquaintances on the cheek or shake hands with, or sit too close to strangers. We knew that too much talking might offend God, and we should "Keep it to ourselves, it wasn't that bad, no one should know if we were happy or sad."

The Warnings

Training and disciplining kids was no easy task, and it called for different strokes for different folks. Some kids automatically got teary-eyed and bawled if somebody looked at them with crossed eyes. Other kids would push the limits and pick one fight after another with their siblings. We knew that actions had consequences and we were usually given some kind of warning.

Warnings were short and to the point. Farm mothers never said, "Wait until your dad finds out about this," because kids knew, and she knew, he wasn't the one who handled the disciplining in the family. Kids weren't given a "time out." Time out was what the boy's basketball team did when they were down two, with two minutes to go.

A warning might just be the gesture of a mother putting her hands on her hips while giving "the look," or shaking an index finger at her kid. Sometimes she just rattled the wooden spoon drawer, and that was enough. A verbal warning might be a mother saying "You fall out of that tree and break your legs, don't come running to me," or "You made your bed, now you are going to lie in it." If a kid threatened to run away from home, most moms said nothing, and it worked.

The punishments – Spare the Rod and Spoil the Child

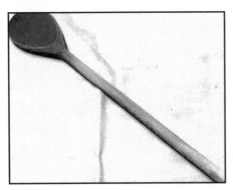

Even though we read in the good book that if you spared the rod you spoiled the child, most of the mothers in Viking Township didn't use a rod. If need be, they used a wooden spoon to paddle behinds. They didn't paddle too hard, but just hard enough so kids would get the point. If kids sassed back to their mothers or were caught using bad words, they invariably had their mouths washed out with a bar of soap. If kids giggled uncontrollably or acted out in church during the sermon, mothers reached under the offending kid's arm and pinched the fleshy skin under the upper arm. Sometimes they would put their arm around their kid's shoulders and nonchalantly pinch an ear lobe.

Training in the Church

Sunday School

One hour every Sunday morning from Labor Day to Memorial Day, children of different denominations gathered in church basements across the nation to sing and learn songs and hymns, to pray silently, to memorize the Ten Commandments and the creed, to watch filmstrips and to hear stories that were told using flannelgraph boards. It was Sunday School time! Many of the "church pillar" parents were the teachers, and not

only did they made sure their kids had their nickels tied in the corner of their hankies for the offering plate, but the night before they quizzed their children to make sure they had their memory work down pat, and their lessons learned.

Vacation Bible School

In the summer, kids went to VBS for two weeks to sing, pray, memorize and do art projects which entailed carving Holy Bibles out of Ivory soap bars and making

and mounting cork crosses on balsam wood. VBS was also taught by the "church pillar" mothers. Those that were pillars but weren't good at teaching, served the nectar and cookies.

Bible Camp

When a child was about nine-to-ten years old they were sent off to Bible Camp where they learned how to live with others in a cabin, eat in a community

LUTHER CREST 8/16-22/59   VERNON STUDIO

diner, swim using a buddy system, pray out loud in front of others and sing lively songs at a nightly church service using actions that bordered on dancing.

By the time kids were considered Juniors (13-year-olds), they were ready to start Confirmation "Reading for the Minister," and were pretty well versed in all the familiar Bible stories. They could sing all the familiar songs, and knew how to pronounce and recite the books of the Bible in order. At this point in their lives, they could recite the Ten Commandments, the Lord's Prayer and the Creeds, but not the meanings. They also had heard all the horror stories about Catechization and Confirmation, and were well aware that the real work was about to began, and there was no getting out of it.

Lutheran kids knew that for two years they would be meeting with the pastor on Saturday mornings not only to study things like faith, grace, sacraments, temptation and justification, but they would also have to memorize countless Bible verses, and second, third and fourth verses of hymns. The "biggie" was the requirement to memorize all of <u>Luther's Small Catechism</u>, all five parts (six if you came from the Missouri Lutheran Church Synod[1]), and having to recite back all the "What does this mean?" and "How is this done?" portions to the pastor.

They also knew they would be sitting together on Sunday morning in the front two pews and taking sermon notes which they had to hand in for the pastor to review.

The most dreaded part of the Confirmation ordeal was Catechization. Two to three nights before Sunday Confirmation Service was held, the Confirmands had to line up in the front of the church and show that they knew their stuff by answering random questions that the pastor asked them in front of parents, siblings, former Sunday School teachers, other parishioners and the Mrs. Snustads of the church. After they made it through catechization in one piece, they knew they could breathe easy and the only thing left to worry about was taking communion for the first time and choking on the wafers and wine. *This is most certainly true.*

We weren't handed out punishments in the Lutheran or other Protestant churches, but we were called into the pastor's office and admonished if we had gone astray. Some pastors threatened to withhold Holy Communion to those he felt had crossed the line. The Catholic parochial kids were given corporal punishment by no-nonsense nuns. The Pope even excommunicated a few that he thought were beyond salvaging.

[1]Many Missouri Synod Lutheran kids went to parochial school and had much more training than the kids who were members of other Lutheran synods. Catholic kids memorized a lot too, but their memorization work certainly didn't come from <u>Luther's Small Catechism</u>. Other Protestant churches didn't make as big of a deal out of Confirmation, and their kids got off pretty easy – especially the Congregationalists.

The Ten Social Commandments

1. **THOU SHALT NOT DANCE FAST OR SLOW.**

2. **THOU SHALT NOT WEAR PANCAKE MAKEUP, DANGLY EARRINGS OR BRIGHT RED FINGER NAIL POLISH.**

3. **THOU SHALT NOT SHOOT POOL OR HANG AROUND THE BILLIARD HALL, GET LEWD TATTOOS OR PLAY WITH FACE CARDS.**

4. **THOU SHALT NOT SMOKE, SPIT OR CHEW (and this includes cloves).**

5. **THOU SHALT NOT CLAP, LAUGH OR CARRY ON IN CHURCH.**

6. **THOU SHALT NOT TELL BARNYARD JOKES OR POSSESS TIMM'S IMPLEMENT SHOP CALENDARS.**

7. **THOU SHALT NOT DRINK ANYTHING STRONGER THAN WHAT THE WCTU FOLKS WOULD.**

8. **THOU SHALT NOT DATE OUTSIDE THE FAITH. (Sometimes this means outside your synod.)**

9. **THOU SHALT NOT GO TO MOVIES OTHER THAN *MARTIN LUTHER* IN BLACK AND WHITE, *THE TEN COMMANDMENTS*, AND *SONG OF NORWAY*.**

10. **THOU SHALT NOT ASSOCIATE WITH ANYONE WHO COMMITS THESE THINGS.**

Note: The social commandments were not memorized, but a code that Norwegian Lutherans lived by and that they passed from the father, to the children, to the third and fourth generation. . .

Put a Slip On,
I Can See Right Through You!

Scandinavian Lutherans in Fish County and elsewhere didn't dress to impress or have a closet full of clothes. We sewed, bought, remade and wore clothes that were practical, sturdy, and morally decent for church and for work. From the cradle to the grave, we knew who would wear what, and when and why. We basically had four different sets of clothes – everyday clothes, barn clothes, church clothes, and "In-Between everyday and church clothes."

Everyday Clothes

Church Clothes

Baby Clothes

Clothes worn by infants – before they took matters into their own hands – and spit back mushy Pablum at anyone who was feeding them, were made of cream-colored wool, flannel and cotton. The hodgepodge of "gender neutral" clothes called layettes included undershirts, diapers, drawstring sacks, kimonos, buntings, bonnets, booties, bibs and swaddling blankets. At the time babies reached the age they were able to stay propped up without tipping over, young toddler girls were dressed in pink or yellow, and the boys were dressed in blue or gray.

Kids' Clothes

By the time toddlers were potty trained, able to walk, and made their disdain for string beans known, they, like goats, were called kids. They were dressed like "mini" adults, but didn't get to pick and choose what they were going to wear.

Church Clothes

Everyday Clothes

Girls wore "good dresses," jumpers, skirts and blouses to church with leather or patent leather shoes. They also had special Christmas dresses made from velvet or taffeta for the Sunday School Christmas Program, and see-thru nylon dresses for Easter. Outerwear at Easter consisted of pastel-colored, "marshmallow-feeling," shorty coats, nylon gloves, and hats with chin straps. If a young girl was in a hurry trying to get her hat on, the chin strap often snapped back and bit her in the neck. Church clothes worn by boys consisted of dark pants, shirts in colors of blue or gray, and a pair of brown or black-colored tie shoes that didn't smell barn.

Girls' school clothes consisted of short-sleeved, Peter Pan-collared, plaid and print cotton dresses, sailor outfits, jumpers, skirts and white blouses that were worn over underpants, undershirts, and slips. In the winter, girls wore corduroy pants under their dresses for warmth, along with long white or brown heavy cotton stockings that were hooked in place by garter belts. Sweaters, coats and heavy-duty kerchiefs tied on heads and over mouths, kept them from seeing their spit freeze in the air. Mittens, clipped to sleeve cuffs, kept the heat in and the cold out. It was all about what modern-day people call "layering." Boy's' school wardrobes consisted of undershirts, t-shirts, cotton shirts, striped knit shirts, dark corduroy pants, overalls, hand-knitted sweaters, parka jackets, snow pants, mittens, scarves and hats with earlaps. Boys' school clothes always looked a little grungy and ill-fitting, but the boys didn't care, and nobody else did either. When kids returned home from school, they had to change into everyday clothes. These clothes were basically worn out school clothes.

Young Adult Clothes

Anyone over the age of twelve knew how to milk and knew how to drive. They were considered young adults who were old enough to know better. About the time young adults started "reading for the minister," the mandatory dress code started to unravel like the hem on a store-bought dress, especially for girls.

By the time girls had been Confirmed, they were wearing nylon hose hooked to garter belts with bow-clipped, three-inch heels to church. They donned can-can slips made from 50-yards of scratchy, tulle fabric under flarey skirts to school. They looked like they were interviewing for the "Lawrence Welk Show." However, the madness didn't end there. After Confirmation was over, girls abandoned their gathered skirts with side zippers that they had made

85

as 4-H projects, and started wearing and wiggling around in straight skirts so tight they could hardly bend their knees.

No matter how many times a Scandinavian Lutheran mother said, "Put a slip on, I can see right through you," fashion, like the world around them, was changing at a dizzying pace. Young girls were bound and determined to change with it, slip or no slip. They "slipped" into bobby socks, penny loafers, saddle shoes and white tennis shoes that they polished and wore with nylons. They wore petti-pants, pantaloons, poodle skirts, capri pants, dungarees, shorty pajamas and bathing suits with boy legs that showed too much skin.

They sported boots called Kickerinos that left an indelible black, chapped line on the back of their legs when they were knee-deep in snow. They took off their heavy wool, winter scarves, and traded them for multi-colored, 16-inch, nylon scarves. They folded them in a triangle and tied them under their chins. If they were "going steady," they tied them on their chins. They also wore them around their neck to cover up hickeys.

Fashionable jewelry consisted of pop beads, charm bracelets, sweater guards, little multi-colored clothes pins that were pinned on Peter Pan collars, Confirmation watches, Luther's Rose pins, or Mary Medallions for Catholics. Post-Confirmation Lutheran girls put away their Sunday School pins that they had earned for perfect attendance, and never wore them again.

Boys who were "Reading for the Minister" basically just wore what their mother told them to wear. They were at an age where their voices hadn't changed, and they enjoyed cracking their knuckles in front of girls. On a dare they would snap a girl's bra who was sitting in the desk in front of them. After they were confirmed, and they had started to shave their "peach fuzz," they began to pay attention and spiff up a bit more. Young men didn't get into the fashion scene like the girls. Boys in Fish County didn't wear white bucks or blue suede shoes like young adult men wore on TV. However, they did take off their bibs, slicked their hair back, and did the best they could to look like they knew that the world was bigger than Fish County.

Church Clothes

Women usually had two church dresses, one for winter and one for spring. They also had two pair of high heels, black heels which they wore between Labor Day and Memorial Day, and white heels which they wore between Memorial Day and Labor Day.

Most men wore suits and ties to church. If it was warm, they took off their jackets, but never their ties. Scandinavian Lutheran men owned four to five suits in their lifetime. Sometimes, a boy's first suit was bought when he was a young kid because he needed it for a special occasion. The second suit was bought for Confirmation, and the third suit was the wedding suit. The fourth suit was bought because they grew out of their wedding suit, and they needed a suit for their daughter's wedding. Their fifth suit, the final one, was bought for their 40th or 50th wedding anniversary, and it was the suit they had on when they were laid to rest.

In-Between and Everday Clothes

When women decided it was time to have a new church dress, their old church dress was relegated down to the "In-between church and everyday" category. These dresses were worn at Sunday School picnics, family reunions, John Deere Day and other events. Once these dresses had seen their better days, but still were too good to throw, they were given to the missions.

For women, everyday clothes were house dresses that were usually sewed using the same pattern over and over again (Simplicity #4849). They were made of cotton floral or checkered prints, and sometimes trimmed with rick rack. Most of them were made with short sleeves, a shirt-style collar, a matching cloth belt and a gathered skirt. The skirt was made long enough so a woman would able to pull it up to rub her eyes and use the hem of it as a hanky in a pinch. House dresses were made ample enough so they could be pulled up and out to gather crab apples in the skirt pouch when a bucket wasn't handy. An everyday house dress could be used as an "In-Between dress" when it was fairly new, but not after underarm sweat stains became visible or the cloth belt was getting too frayed. When an everyday house dress was pretty well worn out, it became a "go to" dress to be worn over milking pants when helping the Mr. yank out the calf of a bellowing cow that was in the middle of a tough delivery. Men's everyday clothes consisted of long-sleeved, cotton shirts, bib overalls and sturdy work pants.

Barn Clothes

Besides worn-out everyday clothes, additional barn clothes consisted of a splattering of old jackets, old storm coats donated by town relatives, milking pants, boots and work gloves. Due to their repugnant smell, barn clothes were quarantined from other clothes and relegated to hang on hooks either in a basement or an entry porch.

Hose, Socks, Shoes, Boots and Overshoes

Scandinavian women were never barefoot except when sleeping, in the hospital or nursing a broken toe. As soon as their feet hit the floor, they put on their shoes and stockings and began their day. They wore two-inch heels to church with seamed-up-the-back nylon hose, wedgies and thick-strapped sandals for "In-Between," and tie glovettes and cotton anklets for everyday. Grandmothers wore black, sturdy tie shoes they tied with long brown stockings that they peeled down below the knee, and rubber-banded in place, when they were hot, or their varicous veins were throbbing. Men's shoes were always in need of polishing and nothing to write home about, unless they had some fancy cowboy boots.

Women had calf-length, black fur-lined boots for winter, and clear plastic button-on-the-side boots they used when the snow was melting, the streets were overflowing, and the heavens opened up the floodgates. They used their husband's 4-bucklers when they were helping in the barn. Men had 4-bucklers for everyday use, and "rubbers" which were low-cut, rubber boots that they slipped on over their shoes and wore to church.

Hats, Caps and Kerchieves

Women wore hats to church, and at Easter they were decked out in Easter bonnets which really weren't bonnets, but pastel-colored hats that had fake fruit, flowers, and netting hanging from them. When the weather wasn't cooperating, they wore a cotton or wool flowered or checked scarf that they folded in the shape of a double triangle and tied under their chin. They wore straw hats in the heat of the day, in the field and out in the barn. Grandmas wore inconspicuous smaller, darker colored hats for church, plastic breeze bonnets for windy days, and heavy wool scarves in the winter. Men never went without a head covering, and only took them off in church, when saluting the flag, or when they needed to get some fresh air on the top of their heads. Hats were basically security blankets for big, grown men. The assortment of head covering men wore ranged from Stetson hats to cowboy hats to wool hats with earlaps to "elevator" caps with logos imprinted on them.

Foundation Garments

Girdles, also known as "good girdles," were only worn on Sunday. They held up nylon hose, and had a tendency to stick to newly-varnished church pews. Corsets, instruments of persecution and tribulation, were used to uplift and firm up the foundation of bodies parts that were sagging, bagging and bulging. They, like girdles, had clamps on them to hold up nylon hose.They were made of bands of elastic that were embedded with bones, hooks and eyes. They were uncomfortable, ill-fitting and irritated the skin.

Slips

Slips, were like summer suasage sandwiches, they came either whole or half. Slips were referred to as a second skin, and were made from white or cream-colored nylon or rayon fabric, and sometimes embelished with lace. They were worn under dresses to prevent dresses from clinging, and to cover up body parts. German Lutheran and German Catholic women who were followers of Lawrence Welk and liked to polka and square dance, wore can-can slips under their dance skirts.

Special Occasion Clothes

Clothes that fell under the special occasion category were baptismal gowns, Confirmation dresses and suits, formals, wedding gowns and veils, military clothes and lettermen's jackets. After they were used, special occasion clothes were folded up, put in a box, stored in the attic, never worn again and never thrown away.

Clothing Accessories

Women's accessories that were everyday staples were hankies and aprons, and all women owned many different styles and types for different occasions. Men's accessories were ties they wore on Sunday, belts to hold up their pants and handkerchiefs. Older men, who needed all the help they could get, used garters to hold up their socks, and suspenders to hold up their belted pants.

Clothing Decorations and Adornments

Most Scandinavian farm women had two pieces of "good" jewelry that they wore daily – their wedding rings, and a watch. When women "gussied up" for special occasions, they sometimes complimented their outfits with three-strand beaded costume jewelry necklaces and matching clip-on earrings. Older women pinned brooches and cameos on their bosoms, and all women wore decorative enameled Christmas pins on their winter coats. Some, but not all, men had a wedding band. However, they all had a watch they wore every day. Some men had tie clasps, but they were rarely used. Both young and old men had a pair of cufflinks in their dresser drawer that somebody had given them as a gift at some time in their lives. The cufflinks stayed in the drawer next to a great-grandfather's pocket watch that never worked, and silver and gold nuggets from the teeth of somebody in the family who had died.

A short Vignette

You are what you wear

One chilly, August Saturday evening when Hilda Thorsrud and Ethel Tronvald were sitting in their car on main street watching people go by, they spotted seventeen-year-old Norma Joy Slette, one from their own flock, wiggling down the sidewalk in a tight skirt, chewing gum and arm-and-arm with a sailor man they didn't recognize. That wasn't the worst of it. She was wearing a tight-fitting Ban-Lon cardigan sweater backwards over a Lana Turner bullet bra. Hilda said to Ethel, "Looks like she's pointing the way straight to hell. Is there no shame left in the world?" Ethel said, "I blame those movie magazines they get at the drug store." Hilda shook her head and replied, "Ya, that could be, but I blame the new Red Hymnals too, and where in the world is her mother, anyway?"

People like Hilda and Ethel were Scandinavian Lutherans, but they weren't born in a barn. Sixty years later, they still could recite the names of the girls in their day and age that acted like Norma Jean Slette and found themselves with a bun in the oven. They knew that Norma Jean Slette's reputation would be remembered by all, and for years to come.

School Days –
Good Old Golden "Ruler Days"

When Viking Township was first platted, the homes and barns were the first buildings to be built, the churches were next, and then came the rural one-room schools. Last, but not least, the little white township hall was built.

The Scandinavian-Americans knew the importance of religion, civics and education, but they had no extra time to sit and read, except for the Bible. They had enough on their plates trying to learn English, pronounce their "J's" and "Th's," milk, clear the land, maintain a garden and keep up with other backbreaking chores.

Some of their children didn't have an opportunity to go past grade eight, and oftentimes that education was spotty. When the weather on the prairie turned nasty and it was too tough for kids to walk four miles up hill each way in the dead of winter in shoes that didn't fit, they just stayed home.

Boys were excused from school in the fall to help with harvest, some had to leave school early to go in the military, and some went to places like the Crookston or Morris Agriculture Schools which were only in operation for six months out of the year. Other girls, like Bertha Hanson, only went through eighth grade because she had to stay home to take care of her mother, Agnes, who was doing poorly, and her brothers. Some girls, like Vivian Anderson, went to high school for two years, but then had to quit because they became "PG" and were sent away.

One day, Arnie Kvitne, who —in tenth grade — sat behind Margaret Kolsrud and spent his time snapping her bra and slumping in his seat, just got up and quit school. He believed he was wasting good time sitting in school because he had convinced himself all it took was common sense and trial-and-error to figure out things in life. Like he told his friend, Roy, "There is more than one way to skin a cat." He ended up owning a butcher shop, and made it through life just fine."

People like Roy Fringstad quit school because they were more into drag-racing, than dangling participles and diagramming sentences. They were referred to as grease monkeys, and they wore the title like a badge of honor. They spent their time underneath a hood of a car self-educating themselves on pistons, spark plugs, carburetors and manifolds. They organized car clubs, and taught each other. They hung around shops that fixed machinery to learn all they could, and their knowledge and abilities became indispensable to farmers who needed their machinery and cars repaired.

Most farmers didn't have a whole lot of schooling, but were smart enough to get much needed education and help from the County Extension Agent and each other. They also organized into farm organizations such as the Farm Bureau, the Farmers Union and the National Farmers Organization to learn new farming methods, fight politicians and to socialize with a little lunch. Women joined Happy Homemakers Clubs that were organized by County Extension Agents to get educated on things such as updated canning methods, making bound button holes and growing bigger dahlias. 4-H Clubs were organized to teach children how to learn by doing, and "make the best better."

In the '50s school consolidation was in full swing. Viking Township District #121 closed down, and the kids were bused to the consolidated school in Otter Falls along with two other rural schools, and the town kids from Herringdal and Otter Falls. This followed months of meetings and rebuilding.

School usually started a few days after Labor Day, and finished about the third week in May. There were two weeks off to celebrate Christmas, and a two-day break at Easter. They weren't called holidays or breaks; they were Christmas and Easter vacations.

School was also let out in October for a few days so the teachers could go to a teachers' convention somewhere in a large city. In good farming years, this coincided with silo-filling and the kids were expected to help out. There weren't any vacation days built into the school calendar year because nobody really went on a vacation. School closed down if the drifts started piling up and the winds drifted the roads shut. If this happened, kids who lived in the country had designated town homes where they stayed. School also was closed for big measles or mumps outbreaks and polio scares, but not for ringworm or chicken pox.

Most started school when they were six years old. Some were five because kids could start school if they turned six before the first of January. Many rural small towns didn't have kindergarten, and there was no preschool. School started at 9:00 a.m., and ended at 4:00 p.m. Town kids walked to school, most school districts had buses for the rural children, and others were driven to school by their parents or neighbors. Once kids, especially farm boys, reached the age of 12 or 13, they often drove themselves to school in an old pickup that had guns in the back so they could hunt birds, rabbits and squirrels on the way home.

Most small-town schools looked about the same. They were two-storied large, brown brick buildings sometimes with a full basement for more classrooms, the boys' and girls' bathrooms, a janitor's room and a furnace room. To enter the building, one had to climb about 16 large steps that were flanked by iron handrails that kids slid down on in the spring, and got their tongues stuck on in the winter. The second floor had a set of rickety metal outside steps that could be used in case there ever was a fire, but there never was, so they were just used for fire drills.

Usually the high school classes were upstairs, seventh and eighth grade classrooms were on the main floor along with the music and home economics rooms. The shop room and basketball locker rooms were either down in the basement or here, there and anywhere. Grades one through six had classrooms on the main floor so they wouldn't get shoved down any steps by the big kids. There was one classroom for each grade, whether it was a small class or large class. In the '50s, each classroom had about 20-38 students who sat alphabetically in desks with inkwells that were no longer used. The walls all had pull-down maps and screens, and pull-down shades on the large-sized windows. The blackboards were called black even if they were the newer green ones.

Most schools had a gymnasium that was used for lyceums, boys' basketball games, PTA meetings, proms, banquets, polio vaccinations, and a place where girls were hauled to hear about what to expect when they got older. These talks were often a year or two too late. The talk was accompanied by a black and white filmstrip about how to hook a Modess — rhymes with "Oh yes" — pad on to a garter-type elastic belt. When the session was over, it was painfully difficult for the girls to look at those they met in the hall, especially those smirky boys.

The hot lunch room was often near the gymnasium. Kids lined up, got their meal cards punched ($2.00 a card for ten punches), and lunch ladies dished up things like mashed potatoes with watery hamburger gravy, barbeques, fish sticks on Friday served with mashed potatoes smothered in watery melted butter, canned string beans, corn or peas, peach or pear sauce, and a choice of either plain or peanut butter bread accompanied by a jar or small carton of milk. Before they quit school, Arnie Kvitne and Roy Fringstad would sometimes try to raise Cain and egged on others to start a food fight in the lunch room, but they always stopped it just before they were caught in the act.

There weren't a lot of choices or variety in high school when it came to class offerings. There were four different classes of math, three or four of science, English and history/government each year, a smattering of business classes — typing, shorthand and basic business, and some home economics and shop classes. Some schools offered two-year foreign language programs, but they were basically a waste of time. There was a lot of homework, but backpacks were only for those on military maneuvers overseas. Students just carried their books stacked up. If books were only one to three years old, kids had to make fake covers out of brown paper bags.

There was quite a bit of memorization in public school. (Perhaps this was because most of the teachers were Lutheran and had had to memorize Luther's Small Catechism prior to Confirmation.) Public school students memorized everything from the "Pledge of Allegiance", the "National Anthem", presidents' names, state nicknames and capital cities in elementary school to the Periodic Table, "The Song of Hiawatha" and Shakespeare quotes in high school.

We learned when Rome fell, and when the Battle of Hastings occurred — 476 A.D. and 1066 A.D., respectively. We were taught about Homer, a really old Greek guy, and had to study his poems, "The Iliad" and "The Odyssey" in which he wrote about really old wars and about men hiding out in the Trojan Horse. He also wrote about Helen of Troy and how beautiful she was, but we couldn't figure out how he'd know because he was blind. What did beauty mean to a blind person? We never asked because good Norwegian Lutherans from Viking Township didn't question anything when it came to school work. We just did what the teacher told us to do. When we got to college we found out that Homer maybe didn't write these lengthy poems, or at least not alone.

Teachers ran the gamut from the good to the bad to the ugly. Their training ranged from Normal School to fully state-certified teachers. There was one superintendent and one principal, and most of them meant business. They acted like drill sergeants, and tried their best to get kids to buck up and graduate. Hoods and really mean upper classmen either flunked or got expelled from school.

In the Beginning there was First Grade

The rules our parents taught us — cleaning up our plates, bodies and souls, sitting up straight, acting decent, being respectful, helping others, and not talking out of line or out of turn — were the same rules we were expected to observe in school.

First grade school teachers were always scary and intimidating to six-year-old girls in print dresses and braids, and to scrubbed up boys in blue dungarees and plaid shirts. Most first grade teachers looked like they were about 100-years-old, and some of them had their hair pulled back in such tight buns they looked like they should be flying a broom or in a framed photo on the wall by Washington.

The first-grade teachers knew that the first few weeks of teaching six-year-olds was like herding cats. For most teachers, it wasn't their first time at bat, and they knew what they had to do. It usually worked out. Ruth Nelson, like all the other teachers who had gone to Normal School, started the first day by getting the kids seated at their desks in alphabetical order, and followed by giving the short kids footstools so their feet wouldn't dangle.

After that, she wrote her name on the blackboard in big letters, pointing at it with the end of a long pointer and said, "My name isn't teacher. You will call me Miss Nelson." Since nobody could read, the kids just looked at her while she continued to talk and fill them in on dos and don'ts. "If you want to go to the bathroom you always have to ask permission. If you have to go #1, raise your hand and hold up one finger. If you have to go #2, raise your hand and hold up two fingers." (Whose business was it anyway?) Since nobody knew where the bathrooms were and nobody dared ask, most just tried to hold it.

She continued, "Everyone has to clean up their plate at noon dinner. You are either a whistler or a whiner. Whistlers clean up their plates, and whiners don't. I don't want to see any whiners in my room."

As the first day went on, the kids were taken on a field trip around the school, and Miss Nelson pointed out — and had them use — the bathrooms. She took them to the lunch room to eat, and took them outside for recess before they all returned to the classroom where she had them put their heads down on their desks to rest for about 15 minutes.

The day progressed with her reading stories, teaching them to sing a song, and doing an art project. She warned them not to eat the paste, and to stay in the lines when coloring. At the end of the first day she got the kids on the right buses, and sent them home with a note for their parents reminding them to bring two blue #2 pencils without erasers, a Big Chief tablet, a fat eraser, a box of eight crayons, and lunch money if they didn't bring a lunch bucket.

As the days went on, the kids knew Miss Nelson would greet them every morning at the door and check their fingernails to make sure they were clean and that they didn't smell barn. They knew what hook to hang their coats on in the cloak room, and knew how to recite the "Pledge of Allegiance." The girls knew if they were good they could be rewarded by being chosen to clean the blackboards and the big erasers. The boys knew if they picked their nose, yanked a girl's braids or threw a spitball, they would either end up standing in the corner with a dunce hat on with their nose touching the wall, or getting their fingers slapped with a ruler. It seems slapping fingers with a ruler was more prevalent in parochial schools, and this action was one of the nuns' guilty pleasures.

Kids learned how to print their names, and all the letters by first writing the letters in the air with their fingers. They were taught how to put the tail between the lines, and knew what the word penmanship meant. First graders were put in reading groups depending upon if they caught on fast, were average, or had a tough time learning. Everyone knew that Group #1 was filled with mostly girls, Group #2 was a mix of boys and girls, and Group #3 was mostly boys. In some schools these were not numbered, but called the Blue, Red, and Green groups. It didn't take long before the phonics lessons kicked in and first graders were reading outloud about Dick, Jane, Sally, Puff, Spot and Tim looking, seeing, running and jumping.

By the end of the year first graders knew a lot of things about two Presidents – Abe Lincoln who had a lot of trouble on his hands, and George Washington who lied about cutting down a cherry tree and was hanging on their wall looking like he was suspended in a cloud. They could tell about the Pilgrims, and who sailed the ocean blue in 1492. They also knew how to put on their thinking caps, how to learn things by heart, and what the letters A, B, through F — with all the pluses and minuses — meant on their report cards. Recess was the favorite time for most kids.

In time, the little kids were introduced to flash cards. They also had 4" X 5" inch dental cards (pink, blue, or yellow depending upon the year) that had to be signed by a dentist. Teachers would compete to see which class returned the most cards, and in how to display them. The favorite design was to have the cards form an oddly shaped giraffe, and the one with the longest neck won.

Some students had a hard time adjusting to school life. There were dental appointments, the public health nurse, shots and vaccines, and hearing and vision tests. If that wasn't enough to scare one, there were fire and civil defense drills. Satellites had come into being, and schools were required to have "duck and cover" exercises to prepare students in case the Communists in Russia decided to drop a nuclear bomb in North Dakota or the surrounding states. Farm kids' designated town homes wouldn't work in such situations. Fire and civil defense drills caused many anxious moments, questions and nightmares.

In time, even the little first graders found themselves in Junior High and High School. One of the best things about these levels was getting a locker. Another was taking part in extracurricular activities. Perhaps the best of all was getting a driver's license... even if one didn't have a car. It was a rite of passage.

Locker numbers were assigned by a mystery person, and usually each class had a row in the same hallway. There were no padlocks for lockers because there was nothing of value in them, except for some leftover lunch and maybe sunflower seeds.

Extracurricular activities in Junior High included band, choir, and sports for the boys: football in the fall, basketball in the winter, and baseball or track in the spring. Girls were not allowed to play sports until federal action in 1972 with the passage of Title IX. Reasons for no female sports ranged from not enough money in the district budget to foolish concerns about future reproductive concerns. If girls were in sports and somehow wrecked their reproductive system, there might not be enough children born to fight the Communists if the Cold War kept up. Girls were cheerleaders! There were only a few, and they were elite town girls who didn't have to head home and do barn chores after school. Apparently, no one figured out that jumping, backflips, standing on shoulders and doing the splits could affect reproductive issues as much as swinging a bat would.

In one small town some men, having coffee at the local café, decided there could be more baseball and football games if the field could be lit. Installing lights was rather expensive for a small town, but the Commercial Club worked with area farmers who still had windmills years after they were needed. Volunteers disassembled and reassembled these at the field, and area electricians volunteered their time to install the lighting. There was a local celebration the night of the first game, and the windmill lights were still in use thirty years later.

Helping to write and assemble the school yearbook (or annual) and the school newspaper were gender-neutral activities although, in retrospect, it seems the editors for both publications were usually girls. The newspaper was rather fun and funny especially when it focused on surveys. Who is your favorite male vocalist? How fast have you driven a car? Who is your least favorite teacher? This last question was always dropped by the newspaper faculty advisor.

Often the band and choir teacher were the same. Lessons often started in the fourth grade with this same teacher.

There were two concerts for each per year for the Junior Choir, Junior Band, Senior Choir and Senior Band — a Christmas one, and a Spring one. The band and choir also performed for graduation and often baccalaureate. Sometimes it was embarrassing to be an alto in the Junior High Choir. First of all, everything was embarrassing in Junior High, and self-confidence was at a low point. Then, in the middle of choir rehearsal, the director would yell, "Altos! You are flat!" Arms of the altos would shift to cover up places.

The best music group of all was the Pep Band. Members got to play for home football and basketball games, and for many away ones. Sometimes Junior High band members got to play in the Pep Band too. Three buses would often travel to away games: the players' bus, the Pep Band bus, and the Rooter bus which involved a minor fee. And the director went along. At least the students in two of the buses sang "99 Bottles of Beer on the Wall" many, many times on these away trips.

There was also a Marching Band. This band played for local parades and Memorial Day. Many bands were invited to the WDAY Band Day in Fargo. That was a big deal. It seems most band students didn't have time for regular classes.

The director, who also taught students how to cork-grease a clarinet and maintain the sheet music library, was also in charge of district and regional contests, from individuals to ensembles to the full band or choir.

Most kids wanted to play the drums. They were loud, cheaper than instruments because the school owned them, and best of all, they were show-offy.

One band director said that if all snare drummers around the world were lined up without drums, it would be the best thing that ever happened!

Drivers' Training was sort of a bust in rural areas. Farm kids often learned to drive in the cow pasture when they were nine or ten years. They graduated to driving the tractor first, pulling a harmless stone-boat for picking rocks, and then pulling the bale wagon. The stronger folks would hoist, toss and stack the bales. After pulling wagons for a season or so, the driver was no longer a novice and became a regular field worker. However, it was a rare parent who would let a child skip school to work in the field. Education was extremely important...especially to the Scandinavians around Herringdal and Otter Falls.

Drivers' Training consisted of about a two-week diversion from Social Studies class in eighth or ninth grade. There was no behind-the-wheel driving. Students skimmed the Drivers' Manual produced by the state. There was no practicing of parallel parking, four-lane driving or passing, but approximately one week of watching black and white filmstrips of car crashes. Many filmed crashes occurred in convertibles, and others in old pick-ups — driven by a teenager — hauling about ten kids in back. A colored film might have had more effect, but black blood paints a gruesome picture, too. There were no automatic transmissions or seatbelts at that time, just "three-on-a-tree", and three or four people in the front seat. Once a student got confirmed and had a driver's license, they could usually date.

A Good Time was had by Most

There were two main holidays besides Christmas that were celebrated in school. One was Valentine's Day where we traded Valentines that we either made or bought. We had to make our own "mailbox" for these. Usually these were decorated shoeboxes. We hated cards with mushy sayings like "Be Mine," and instead gave cards that just read "Happy Valentine's Day" or "Best Wishes." We ate hard, little, heart-shaped, pastel-colored candies, and sometimes we received extra candy to eat, but none of us had a clue as to who St. Valentine was or where he hailed from — probably because he was Catholic. We found that out when we were older.

The other holiday celebrated in school was Halloween. We dressed up in costumes. The girls usually dressed up as witches or gypsies, the boys dressed up as hobos or cowboys, and both sexes sometimes dressed up as white sheet ghosts with slits cut for the eyes. We got a little candy in school, and sometimes had a little parade around the schoolyard but that was about it. Norwegian Lutheran kids didn't know that Halloween had started as All Saints Day because we didn't know what a saint was or have any in our churches. Catholic kids had saints, but they were more excited about the candy at Halloween than having to pray for dead people who were designated as saints.

Minor holidays we celebrated in school were May Day, Columbus Day and Leif Ericsson Day. We didn't really celebrate, but learned about these days.

For May Day, we again had no clue what we were celebrating, but we made May Baskets as an art project, and there was candy involved.

We had studied about Columbus and knew the names of his ships, and learned a song about "The Nina, The Pinta, The Santa Maria" and sailing in the ocean blue in 1492.

Leif Ericsson was more important, but late to the scene even though he discovered America first. We didn't hear about him until we were in Junior High. A few elementary children had learned a joke from their grandpa and it spread around school. "What did the Indians say when Columbus landed in America?" "*Er det du*, Columbus?" Some teachers thought this joke was very funny, and probably gave those students an "A" for the year.

Ericsson was a Viking and Norse, and therefore very important. We found out later that just because he was Norse didn't mean he was Norwegian. He might have been, but he grew up in Iceland and founded the first Norse settlement in Greenland. We were proud of him, though, and never heard any stories about him beating up people, taking them hostage or pillaging. He probably loved his family, ate *lefse* and behaved like the Norwegian-Americans in Viking Township.

Homecoming wasn't a holiday, but it was an important time in the life of the school. Homecoming was started as a tradition to bring back former students to celebrate the school. Most former students in Midwestern towns didn't show up for homecoming, but made an effort to show up ten years later for a class reunion. Those that were pregnant, divorced, or thought they were too fat, too bald, or hadn't amounted to much, usually were no-shows at the ten-year reunion, and hoped they would win the lottery by the time the next reunion rolled around so they could show everybody up.

The night before the big football game, some schools had additional homecoming activities which included a snake dance. The snake dance didn't have anything to do with either snakes or dancing, but it was an activity where the students held hands while running up and down the streets and alleys in town with no real purpose in mind.

Sometimes there was a bonfire after the snake dance, but nobody knew why because nobody ever burned anything in effigy or roasted marshmallows or weenies at the bonfire.

On the day of the big game, there was a parade. Led

by majorettes, the Marching Band came first, followed by the queen and her attendants in a convertible. Next came a series of pickups pulling crepe paper and chicken wire bedecked hayracks rolling  down the street. There usually was a school dance after the game in the school gymnasium, and Lutherans who didn't know how to dance showed up and just "wall-flowered" it. If it was a sock-hop, meaning the gym floor had been refinished in the last ten years, Lutheran kids leaned against the gym walls in their socks. A good time was had by all.

Many schools chose a queen and king from the senior class who were paraded out at half-time during the homecoming football game. The queen was usually a pretty girl who lived in town and was popular. The king was usually the football captain.

The queen, with her rhinestone crown and wand made from a tin-foil-covered baton, was escorted to the center of the football field by the king. Everybody clapped, and that was about it. The royal court, which consisted of two attendants for the queen and two attendants for the king, were also paraded out at this time. After the homecoming activities had finished, the queen and king had no further "royal" duties. Some schools had prom kings and queens, but for most schools, one queen and king was enough.

Some schools held carnivals for fun and funds. Sometimes they held them because it had become a tradition, sometimes it was a necessary evil, and sometimes they became more work than they were worth. Pity the poor parents who worked behind the "fishpond" curtain.

Throughout the year, Friday evenings were the time we attended any number of team baseball or softball games in the summer, and watched the boys play basketball in the winter. It was the closest thing to a public display of emotion, school pride and loud-noise celebrating anybody had ever witnessed. The band would egg everyone on while playing the Otter Fall Otters' fight song, the cheerleaders with their bullhorns led the cheer — "*Lutefisk, lefse, fattigmann og snus*, You don't know it, but you're going to lose." Even parents went a little haywire and were yelling to beat the band.

When Anton Hauge's son, Jerry, shot the winning bucket at the buzzer, and the Otters were propelled into the Class B basketball team state tournament, Anton became so emotional he hugged his wife smack-dab right in front of everyone in the bleachers. Even some kids saw it. This was truly a red-letter day, and one for the history books for the whole community.

People looked forward to graduation just as much as most had looked forward to first grade.

But learning — like life — went on, and for various reasons it didn't always take place in a school building. One didn't have to go to school to be a politician or a car salesman. One just had to know how to turn up the heat, pull some strings, and pull the wool over the people's eyes.

Graduates who had second thoughts about farming, or didn't have a farm to inherit, went to into the military or to

Minneapolis or Fargo to find employment.

°Those who were still trying to find themselves went to:
  --Normal School to learn how to teach,
  --Trade schools to learn to fix up machines and
    people, mechanical and beauty courses,
  --Nursing school to learn how to give shots and
    properly make beds,
  --Business colleges to learn secretarial skills, banking
    or auctioneering,
  --Lutheran and other liberal Arts colleges with
    mandatory Basic Bible and Christian Doctrine
    classes because they were pressured to attend
    someplace with a wholesome atmosphere and a
    good choir,
  --Lutheran Bible or Moody Bible Institutes to keep
    others on the straight and narrow, and
  --State universities for a whole host of other
    programs like Home Economics

°People that were smarter than a whip studied to be:
  --Doctors so they could treat people with every
    imaginable ailment,
  --Veterinarians so they could treat animals with every
    imaginable ailment,
  --Dentists so they could torture people,
  --Lawyers so they could handle disputes between
    people who had an ax to grind, and charge people
    an arm and leg for not understanding what they
    needed to understand, and
  --Pastors or priests.

The second and third generation of Scandinavian-Americans had acquired their ancestors' love of reading and education. Each home in Viking Township had some form of family library; some books, subscriptions to farming magazines and the county newspaper, "Fish County Weekly," and usually a subscription to a newspaper from a major city like the "Minneapolis Tribune" or the "Fargo Forum."

The most popular magazines seemed to be: "Successful Farming", "The Farm Journal," "The Farmer," "Popular Mechanics," "Ladies Home Journal," "Life," and "National Geographic."

Some magazines and newspapers were shared with the neighbors, and it was often Dougie Johnson's job to deliver these.

Plighting Thee My Troth

Norma Jean Stokke sewed her own bridal gown and veil. Her bridesmaids were her sisters Betty Lou and Carol Ann. They sewed their own dresses, and Norma Jean made the flower girl dresses for her nieces. Norma Jean's mother, Alice, sewed her own dress, as well as Norma Jean's "going away" dress. There was just a lot of talent in that family. The "glads" were grown on the farm, and the other flowers were ordered from the mortician in town. The Altar Guild furnished the tapers and got the altar all set up. Olmstad's Photography took the photos. They were the only photography studio within 75 miles so everyone who lived within 75 miles relied on them. They always did a nice job, and were pretty reasonably priced. The women of Norway Lutheran served the lunch. Everything went off without a hitch. "This is most certainly true."

Celebrating Anniversaries

25th Anniversary

Made by Mrs. Ole Svensgaard for Orlin and Aslaug Grimsrud's 25th.

Roshols' 40th: Olga and Ralph Olga didn't get a Ruby, but she did get a corsage. She said Ralph was her "gem," and that was good enough for her.

50 Years of Wedded Bliss

Mr. Lillegaard was a quiet man and didn't like to be put in the limelight. He was just thinking how nice it would be if he were home in his recliner. He didn't even notice that the tapers were tipping.

The Neilsons' were told to stand still and smile for the photo-op. They stood still, but smiling for photos didn't come naturally, so they didn't.

Plighting Thee My Troth

In the '40s and '50s, most people who lived in the country and in small towns were married. The "till death do us part" vow they took usually held up until one of them returned to dust. There was no such thing as a destination wedding. Weddings were held in churches, parsonages, homes or courthouses.

There were various reasons that some people never tied the knot. Some women were so busy taking care of their bachelor brothers and aging parents that they didn't have time to look for a partner. Some men were too odd or too shy to even think about looking for a helpmeet. Olaf Arnegaard never married because, as he said, "I get hen-pecked enough as it is in the brooder house. Vi, on top of dat, vould I need a voman to da the same ting, den?" Hiram Berg, who didn't go to church, had all the benefits of marriage without the commitment. He once told his neighbor, "Why would I buy the cow when the milk is free?"

Dating and courtship

Dating and courtship in rural America changed dramatically between the decades of the 1920's–1930's to the 1940's–1950's. Because people came from the same valley in Norway and immigrated to the same place in the Midwest, it wasn't unusual for shirt-tailed relatives to "tie the knot." However, they usually had no clue they were related. Men usually courted and married a girl that was ten years younger, unless they had to resort to a mail-order bride which meant they couldn't be so picky. It only made sense to look for a helpmeet in the township, and if you found one, you were considered lucky. However, not everybody was lucky.

***It got to be really tough sledding for the Setesdal boys
to find a wife in the woods.***

Courting Customs before and after World War I

Emil Hanson (1890-1942), who farmed 120 acres of wheat and rye on the prairie, had a string of bad luck before he found his Mrs. One cold, Saturday night in '25, Emil changed out of his barn clothes, took a bath, and went to a local barn dance to see Si Perkins and His Cornhuskers perform, and to look for a wife. He was Lutheran so he didn't know how to dance, what to say or how to act around a woman. However, it didn't take long for him to find out.

He spotted a girl who looked both Norwegian and decent. She was standing by herself, so he thought, well, it's now or never. He mustered up all his courage, walked over to where she was standing, cleared his throat, looked down at the floor and said, "I suppose you wouldn't dance with me, then?" When she just looked away, Emil got nervous, so he thought maybe a compliment would work. So, he blurted out, "Ya, for a fat girl, you sure don't sweat much." Well, you know the rest of the story, but he didn't give up.

The next week, with planting season just around the corner, he did the next best thing and placed an ad in the "Lutheran Herald" for a mail-order bride. The ad read:

> *Needed: One sturdy and hefty woman with a strong back. Must know how to work hard and cook for her man without complaining. Need by spring planting.* Swedes need not apply. Please send a recipe.

He only received one reply, and she showed up at his door with a crock of sauerkraut in hand. In her thick, German accent, she told him her name was Heidi Schmidt, she wasn't Swedish, she could work and she could cook. Her nonstop, idle chatter made him nervous, so he sent the black moustache-lipped German woman out the door and on her way.

However, he was bound and determined to keep going. The next week, he placed an ad in the "Decorah Posten" so only Norwegian-speaking women would be able to read it. His ad read:

> *Kjære, Herre Gud, De som alting veit; Vil du skuffa meg ei kjerring, Som er både tjuk og feit!*

(Dear Lord God, You know everything. Will you send me a woman who is both thick and fat?) God answered his prayers. Three days after the ad came out, Bente Benson who lived three miles west as the crow flies from the Hegland homestead near Decorah, IA, showed up at his doorstep with a "termos" of egg coffee and a *tine* full of lard doughnuts. She was everything he needed. She was thick, she was sturdy, she could cook and she could milk faster than the hired man. Yup, the third time was the charm. She was as solid and steadfast as Dover, and agreed to take up housekeeping for him. They went to the courthouse, and Emil paid $2.50 to make it legal. When they got home, he picked her up and carried her over the barn door threshold.

Courting Customs during and after World War II

In '42, when young men were getting drafted and sent off to fight in World War II, courtships were brief, hasty and hurried. The young men didn't know if they would come back with limbs or life intact, and the young women thought they might be too old to get married once the war was over. So, the courthouses were busy issuing marriage licenses, and the parsonages were full of couples who barely knew each other plighting their troth in front of preachers, judges and two witnesses.

Proposals such as "How would you liked to be buried in the family plot, then?" and "Well, it looks like it's now or never," were accepted and worked. Those who didn't have time to find a local before being shipped away, often surprised everyone when they came home with a woman they had met overseas. These women were always referred to as "war brides" up until their dying day. These marriages oftentimes encountered rough sledding and had similar outcomes to "mail-order" bride marriages of the '20s.

Soldiers, who hadn't bothered to get married before they were shipped off and thought they could find a sole heiress to a section of land within driving distance of their land upon returning, were in for a big surprise. They quickly realized they were up against a whole platoon of Rosie the Riveters who believed it was either their way or the highway.

Courting Customs in the '50s

Life returned to normal five years after the soldiers returned home from World War II, and before Sylvania Blue

Dot Flashbulbs were causing people to see spots in front of their eyes.

Courtships became more complicated, time-consuming and out-of-the-norm. Rings containing ¼ carat diamond stones were ordered from Sears-Roebuck and Montgomery Ward catalogs. It was rumored that if push came to shove, some "Farmers in the Dell" took their cues from Hollywood movies and got down on one knee to seal the deal.

Mixed marriages were cropping up like invasive weeds in a potato field that were impossible to control and no amount of DDT would eradicate them. Norwegians with names like Olsons were marrying Swedes with names like Anderssons. Norwegian girls who had married German men were submitting recipes for sauerkraut in church cookbooks. It even got so bad that once in a while an O'Malley from the Holy Name of the Blessed Virgin Mary Parish on the Prairie, who didn't know how to finish the Lord's Prayer, married an Olson from *Nordland* Lutheran Church. If this happened, the one who wasn't inheriting a farm agreed "to turn," and the wedding wasn't a public event, that's for sure.

The Nuptials and all the Work

Nuptials usually took place in late spring or early summer when there was a lull between planting season and harvesting. Sometimes couples got married after harvest and duck hunting season, but before people got too busy banking the house and putting tire chains on their sedans. December weddings were discouraged due to conflicts with Sunday School Christmas Programs, *Lutefisk* Suppers, and all the obligatory nonstop Christmas baking and butchering that needed to get done. Due to the weather, anyone who decided to get married in January or February was just plain foolish, lacked all common sense and usually reaped what they sowed.

Save the Date: Braaten/Stokke Style

Merle, sitting by Norma Jean, trying to get up his nerve to tell his parents they were going to get married.

It was a rainy, April evening when Merle brought his future bride, Norma Jean Stokke, out to the farm to tell his folks that they were going to get married. Merle and Norma Jean were both going to be graduating from Ag School in May, and they had decided to get married the end of June. Merle was kind of nervous. His folks had never met her, and he knew they'd be surprised when he told them the news.

As soon as they got inside the house, Merle introduced Norma Jean to his folks, Harold and Ethel. After they had all shaken hands, Ethel steered them into the living room, pointed to the davenport, and said, "You two sit down here, then." Merle sat down so close to Norma Jean that his mother got all nervous. He knew he needed to start the conversation so he cracked his knuckles, looked at his parents who were sitting in chairs across the room, and began to talk.

Merle: "How about that rain, then?"
Ethel: "Have you ever seen the beat?"
Harold: "It sure came down hard."

Norma Jean: "It rained to beat the band where my folks live, too."

Merle wasn't paying attention to the conversation because he knew he had to tell his parents he was getting married, and that wasn't going to be easy. Right then and there, he made up his mind that it was best to get it over with before they would start asking him questions that could throw him off. So, he took a deep breath, blurted it out and hoped for the best.

Merle: "We're going to bite the bullet so we thought its best we let you know. She comes from around those lakes north of Otter Falls, and her folks got about three inches last night."

Harold: "Has it been dry up there, too?"

Norma Jean: "My dad said it hasn't been this dry in ten years."

Ethel: "What is the name of the church your people go to, then?"

Norma Jean: "Norway Lutheran Church."

Merle: "It's just two miles north of their farm."

Norma Jean: "We will be getting married there the end of June."

Ethel: "I'll go get lunch on. You folks just sit and visit."

Without saying a word, Harold got up from his chair and followed Ethel out of the room. A few minutes later, he came back with the Fish County Plat Book in his hands. He sat down, studied it for awhile, looked up and spoke.

Harold: "Do your relations farm next to the Flatgaards?"

Norma Jean: "Yes, they're my people on my dad's side."

Merle: "Norma Jean was Fish County Dairy Princess two years ago. I meet her at the county fair."

Harold: "I think some of your relations were on the same

119

threshing crew when I was a young buck."

Norma Jean: "You'll get to meet them at the wedding. They all live around there."

Harold: "It was dry as a bone back then, too."

Merle: "It sure is a small world. Who would have thought."

Norma Jean: "I can't wait to tell my dad you knew him."

Harold: "We need a couple of really good soakers like this one in the next couple of weeks if the wheat is going to head out when it's due."

Norma Jean: "I just hope it doesn't rain the day we get married."

Merle's grandma was right. He did have a little bit of devil in him. Merle thought, what the heck, and decided to rattle his dad a little bit. Before he spoke, he reached over and patted Norma Jean's hand and said,

Merle: "Oh you'll look pretty, come rain or shine."

Harold, clearing his throat: "In '34, it was as dry as a bone."

(Ethel, who had been listening to the whole conversation from the kitchen, decided it was probably getting to be too much for Harold. She yelled from the kitchen.)

Ethel: *"Vær så god."*

Harold, Merle and Norma Jean all got up in unison and joined Ethel in the kitchen. After everyone sat down, Ethel apologized for not having much on hand to serve. After they finished eating some dried beef sandwiches she served along with a dish of plum sauce, bars and coffee, Merle spoke:

Merle: "No, its best we get back to school."

Ethel: "Let me pack a lunch for you in case you get stuck."

After they got through their awkward handshakes and they pulled out of the driveway, Harold went and checked the rain gauge for the fourth time that day. When he got back in the house, Ethel was clearing the lunch off the table.

Ethel: "She seemed nice enough, I suppose."

Harold: "Flatgaard blood is good stock. They know how to work."

Ethel: "Well, hopefully Merle knows what he is doing."

The Church/Community Shower

Like all upcoming brides in Fish County, Norma Jean was "feted" with a shower that was given by the ladies of her church. The shower was held in the basement of Norway Lutheran, and the place was plumb full of people from her church, in addition to neighbors, relatives and school friends. The guests showed up with gifts of dishtowels, crocheted potholders, wooden spoons, Pyrex mixing bowls and many other useful things she would need. The event included games, readings, a clarinet solo and a vocal solo. The ladies served a dainty lunch of frosted, olive-garnished sandwich loaves, glorified rice, cake, coffee and lemonade.

Wedding Preparations

Norma Jean altered the neckline. It was too low cut for her taste.

Six weeks before Norma Jean and Merle's upcoming betrothal was announced, and even before the church shower, the real behind-the-scenes work had begun. The Singer sewing machines were oiled well, and tuned up. Norma Jean and her mother, Alice, bought satin, lace and netting fabrics , notions and

Simplicity Pattern #1461 so they could sew the "Oh Perfect Love" wedding gown and finger-tip veil.

The four Stokke women made all the clothes for the bridal party, along with the aprons for the punch servers, and the ladies that worked in the kitchen. They kept the sewing machines humming, and the electric irons turned on and heated up.

The work didn't just revolve around the sewing machine! Norma Jean had to contact the church organist to play, and her youth choir friend to sing "Entreat me not to leave thee" and other songs. She had to write a letter to her roommate from the Crookston Ag School to ask her if she would "man" the guest book. She had to call on two of her neighbor girls to ask them to serve the punch, and two of her 4-H friends to open and display the gifts. She enlisted her mom's best friend to "pin on" all the boutonnieres and corsages. One of her aunts and one of Merle's aunts, were thrilled that she asked them to pour the coffee. The job of cake-cutting went to their godmothers, and she had to fill them in on the details. She called and hired Mrs. Ole Svensgaard to make and deliver the three-tiered white, wedding cake. They had to put in an order for nut cups, and had to mold and make the mints in Norma's colors of blue and yellow. There was no end to all the details she needed to work out. Merle just went along with all of it, and was thankful he didn't have to figure out any of that stuff.

Norma Jean ordered all the flowers and the invitations from the mortician who handled those kinds of things in town. Olmstad's Photography was called and told to put the date of June 25, 1955 on the calendar. Like most rural families in the area who hired Olmstad's to photograph their wedding, Norma Jean wanted him to take some family photos, and at least the eight standard 8" x 10" black-and-white important photos that he took at all weddings.

After all these details were taken care of, the real work was set in motion and continued up until the day of the wedding. Cleaning for Norma Jean's upcoming wedding was much more intense than the cleaning that they did for her Confirmation.

Everything in the house and outside the house, including the manure scrapers and outhouse, had to be cleaned, bleached, hosed down, scraped, painted and spiffed up. They attacked unpleasant odors from mothballs, moldy curdled food in slop pails and the lingering barn smell with elbow grease and whatever it took to eradicate them. By the time the wedding day came, the women were all pooped out from all the planning and the work that went with it.

When the afternoon of the wedding day finally arrived, it was, as Mrs. Jens Stokke said to her daughter, "High time we get on our foundation garments and get this over with, once and for all."

On July 25, 1955 at 7:00 p.m., the Stokke/Braaten wedding nuptials began at Norway Lutheran. After the whole bridal party had marched down the aisle and went to their proper places, Pastor A.E. Hanson started the ceremony. His wedding sermon was not about love, happiness or contentment, but it was filled with stern warnings about trials, tribulations and tough times. Merle, Norma Jean and everyone else in the congregation didn't really listen to it because they had heard the same sermon at every wedding, and many times over.

After the last song was sung and the last prayer was given, Pastor A.E. Hanson pronounced the blessing and the newly-wedded Mr. and Mrs. Merle Stokke held hands and smiled at each other as they headed back down the aisle. Since everyone knew each other, there was no need for a receiving line. Besides, it would make everyone feel awkward, so everybody filed down to the basement to visit, drink some punch, and watch the couple cut the cake. After the cake-cutting was over, everyone got in line to get their finger-sandwiches, cake, nuts, mints and coffee. About 8:45 p.m., everyone was done eating, and the women went to the gift table to look at the gifts and size up what their neighbors and friends had spent.

In the kitchen the church basement ladies, who were on duty, had already started to wash the dishes and wipe down the counters, when Merle and Norma Jean went out to look at their car. The bridal couple jumped into the car for the obligatory photo after they surveyed the string of rusty cans that were attached to the back bumper, and the "Hot Springs Tonight" and "Just Married" slogans that were written all over the car in white shoe polish. They only hoped and prayed that nobody had put Limburger cheese on the manifold.

Servers at Norma Jean and Merle's wedding were all neighbors. Norma made them aprons as a gift.

The bridal couple left the church and went back to the Stokke homeplace where Norma Jean changed out of her dress and into her "going away dress," and Merle changed out of his "monkey suit" and into some normal pants, a comfortable shirt and boots. Finally, about 9:30 p.m., they were on their way to a lake cabin, a favorite place for Minnesotans to honeymoon.

Merle and Norma Jean caught all these fish on their honeymoon. They are pictured with two locals who knew the lake like the back of their hands. These locals told them where the fish were biting. Talk about hitting the jackpot!

Postscript:

Lutheran wedding nuptials were usually held on a Saturday night, and started about 7:00 p.m. The wedding songs that were sung, the sermons that were preached, the flowers that were chosen, the clothes that were worn, and the meals that were served in the church basements were basically the same, no matter if couples were married in Norwegian Lutheran Churches, Swedish Lutheran Churches or Wesley Methodist Churches.

It was a little different with Catholics, who were sometimes referred to as RC's. Usually, their weddings were held in their churches at 10:00 a.m. followed by drinking beer and big roast beef, corn, mashed potatoes and gravy dinners. They wrapped up with wild wedding dances at VFW or Knights of Columbus Halls. The celebrations ended before morning milking, and before 7:00 a.m. mass began.

Honeymoon Hotspots in Minnesota
The Lakes

Because Minnesota is the home to 10,000 lakes (11,842 to be exact), it was just a given that most newlyweds from

Minnesota went to the lakes for their honeymoon. Many of them chose to stay close to home at "Ma & Pa Kettle" type resorts that had about ten small cabins complete with "modern housekeeping." (As far as we can tell, modern housekeeping meant you had indoor toilets, running water, and somebody had already made your bed. It didn't necessarily mean you had both hot and cold water, just running water.)

Amenities included the use of a small fishing boat (motors cost extra, but minnow buckets came with the boat), use of the shack to clean the caught fish, and a little store that sold tackle, Dinty Moore stew, Spam, Campbell's Pork and Beans, Grain Belt beer, milk and Mounds candy bars.

Itasca Park and Bemidji

Some honeymooners went to Itasca Park to walk across the rocks at the source of the Mississippi River, and to Bemidji to see the holy grails of Paul Bunyan and Babe the Blue Ox, two pilgrimages that were 24 miles apart. In '37 Norman Balsrud and his Mrs. were there to see Babe brought into town on a Grinol's Implement and Fuel Company truck arranged so that its exhaust exited through Babe's nostrils. Talk about excitement! People cheering all over!

Duluth

Anyone who lived anywhere in Minnesota and didn't like to sweat, usually made at least one trek to Duluth to see

Lake Superior, the aerial lift bridge, and the Viking ship in Leif Erikson Park. The journey always included a drive up the North Shore to see Gooseberry Falls and the Split Rock Lighthouse. Many Norwegian-American honeymooners went to Duluth because they just accepted their lot in life that they would probably never get to either coast to see an ocean, or over to Norway to see a Viking Ship or a waterfall. They were just thankful they could see something they felt was the next best thing.

Minneapolis/St Paul

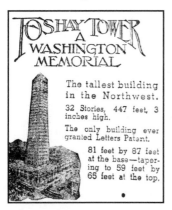

FOSHAY TOWER
A
WASHINGTON
MEMORIAL

The tallest building in the Northwest.

32 Stories, 447 feet, 3 inches high.

The only building ever granted Letters Patent.

81 feet by 87 feet at the base—tapering to 59 feet by 65 feet at the top.

•

Minnesotans and Dakotans who lived on rural routes and honeymooned in the Twin Cities, usually stayed at either the Curtis or Andrews Hotels in downtown Minneapolis, took a tour of the Foshay Tower (the tallest building in the northwest) and looked at Minnehaha Falls. Then they motored over to St. Paul to see the capital building, and the Minnesota State Fairgrounds. If a honeymooning couple were Catholic, they went into the Cathedral of St. Paul, put a dollar in a box and lit a candle for their relatives who had died. If a "Just Married" couple were Lutheran, they bought two chocolate malted milks at Smiley's Point on *Snus* Boulevard for $1.00 before crossing over into St. Paul. After visiting the Twin Cities, honeymooner Martin Ostby said to his Mrs., "Good night, how could you breathe living like that? They're packed in tighter than they are in a can of sardines."

North Dakota Honeymoon Hot Spots

The people who settled and lived in sparsely-populated North Dakota, had no problem living, working and toiling in a place that was known for its harsh winters, brutal summer heat, and endless dust storms where the winds never let up. Otherwise, they would have left. Because all they did was work and go to church, it was no surprise that they never knew what it was like to be wined, dined, pampered or entertained. However, when they were married, many of them did take two to three days to go on a honeymoon. They invariably chose, like their barn cats, to stay pretty close to home. For Norwegian Lutherans, honeymoons were never a "show and tell" event.

Fargo

Even though it was a lot more expensive to go on a "Frolic in Fargo Honeymoon" than to honeymoon at Pine Breezes Lake Resort, there were some couples, who in a weak moment, threw common sense out the window and opted for Fargo. When you were spending your honeymoon at the Gardner, the Donaldson, or any other reputable downtown Fargo hotel where the likes of Carl Ben Eielson, James J. Hill and Lawrence Welk stayed and ate, you were "putting on the Ritz." Eating at the hotel's restaurants rather than at a diner or from a lunch box, wasn't something that a person would do under normal circumstances.

Fargo was an interesting place for rural folks to honeymoon who wanted a once-in-a-lifetime experience to explore a big city. It was a city with nice hotels, lots of churches, a few flop houses, and a dizzying array of stores equipped with all sorts of wonders of the seven worlds. When Ronald Ringdal and his Mrs. went to Fargo for their honeymoon, they acted like little kids and hoped they didn't run into anyone they knew. They rode up and down the

escalators at the F.W. Woolworth's Store, looked at their feet light up like Christmas bulbs in an x-ray machine at the Herbst Department Store, and watched their money go crisscrossing the ceiling in a pneumatic tube at the A.L. Moody's Department Store.

The entertainment didn't stop there. After a day of exploring, the newlyweds agreed that Fargo had it all! However, the honeymoon highlight for Ronald Ringdal and his new Mrs. was sitting at the Fargo Theatre eating popcorn, drinking grape Nesbitt pop, and eating fudgsicles while watching John Wayne and Donna Reed in the movie, "They Were Expendable." Talk about a treat they'd never forget!

Rugby and the Peace Gardens

Honeymooners motoring across North Dakota on old Highway 2, anywhere between Grand Forks and Minot, passed the time by looking at all the "Think" signs that were standing in the ditch. The site-seeing options, which were few and far between, included driving around to look at fields, fishing in Devil's Lake, taking a picture of the World Obelis which was located at the North America National Geographical Center of the World in Rugby, ND, listening to the weather coming from a staticy-sounding radio station out of Winnipeg, Canada, and putting a quarter in the "hooked to the box spring" Magic Finger Relaxation machine to shake the motel mattress for fifteen minutes. For more excitement, some honeymooners motored an hour north on Highway 3 to the International Peace Gardens at the United States Canadian border to look at the planted petunias, the Turtle Hills which were called mountains, and to put their foot in Canada to say they honeymooned out of the country.

The Badlands

For those who wanted to get off the prairie and see some canyons, buttes, gullies, ravines, rattlesnakes and red rocks, the Badlands was the place to go. Coupled with rodeos, round-ups, ranches and real cowboys, it was a boot-kicking, yippee-ki-yay North Dakota honeymoon hotspot for many.

In '46, Lester Holmgren, from Carrington, ND, talked his bride, Thelma, into going to the Badlands for their honeymoon. It was a hard sell, because the Badlands were 250 miles away and she didn't like being that far away from home. She finally relented when he promised her they could stop in Bismarck to look at the capitol building and stay in a real hotel for one night.

When they were about 120 miles out of Bismarck, and the red rocks and buttes were in full view, Lester pulled over to the side of the road and wanted to do a little exploring. He got out of the car, went down the ditch and told Thelma he was going to climb a nearby butte. He said, "Take a picture when I wave, then." Meanwhile, Thelma had to go to the bathroom so bad she had no choice but to "go" behind their car if you know what is meant by that. She no sooner had taken out her Brownie Kodak to get ready to snap a photo of Lester, when she saw him slip on something and roll down a hill.

To make a long story short, Lester crawled back to the car, and was just plain lucky that the only mishaps he had were losing his pocket protector and badly spraining his right ankle. It could have been a lot worse. Thelma had to use a rope to pull his cowboy boot off his swollen foot. As she was tugging on the rope, she fell down, and in the process she dirtied up the seat of her new daisy-printed pedal pushers, and tore many dime-sized holes in both the elbows of her three-quarter length white blouse. Her elbows were not only bloodied, skinned up and full of gravel, but she didn't have any Carbo Salve, adhesive tape or gauze packed in her train case or in the cubby hole to clean up her wounds. To boot, Lester couldn't put any weight on his foot, so they had no choice but to turn around and cut their honeymoon short. Thelma, who wasn't used to driving, had to drive all the way back to Carrington. You can say that this marriage didn't start out on a good foot, that's for sure.

Iowa Honeymoon Hotspots

The Little Brown Church in the Vale – a small, quaint Congregational Church which was located out in the middle of nowhere – was the place to get married if you wanted a small fuss-free wedding, you didn't want anyone to know you were getting married, you were entering into a mixed marriage, or you found yourself in the dilemma of having to have a shotgun wedding. Even if couple didn't get married at the church, it was a favorite place for honeymooners to visit, and everybody knew how to sing the song that was written about the church.

Couples also honeymooned at the Amana Colonies so they could see where their Amana deep freezers were made. It was a strange place for a honeymoon because the old world Germans who lived there considered marriage a spiritual weakness.

Lake Okoboji was the perfect honeymoon spot for those who liked to fish, lie down on a blanket under a tree by the lake and look up at the clouds during the day, and eat cotton candy and ride the Ferris wheel at Arnold's Park in the evening.

Wisconsin Hotspots for Honeymooners
The Dells

 Wisconsin honeymooners who didn't mind being surrounded by a bunch of strangers sometimes chose The Wisconsin Dells as their honeymoon destination. The area was loaded with convenient, enticing drive-up-to-your-door cinderblock motels with exotic names such as The Indian Trail, Dells Gateway and Dick's Sierra Inn. A few of the motels even had outdoor swimming pools like they had in Hollywood and Las Vegas. "Drawing cards" to honeymoon at "The Dells" included, The Tommy Bartlett Thrill Show which featured skimply-clad ladies showing off their water-skiing tricks, duck boat rides down Lake Dalton and the Wisconsin River, and souvenir shops filled with knick knacks, fudge, postcards, and View-Master cardboard disks showcasing the important sites.

Because Wisconsin was also the home to the Blue Mound Cave, a bizarre House on the Rocks, Little Norway, and Door County where locally picked fruit and freshly caught fish were eaten, there were many options for those who honeymooned in Wisconsin. Lutherans who honeymooned in Wisconsin couldn't believe the amount of beer the locals drank right out in the open.

South Dakota Honeymoon Hotspots
The Corn Palace: The "Castle" on the Prairie

Many "Just Married" couples made the east-west pilgrimage across South Dakota, starting at Sioux Falls and ending up in Rapid City, with only a little help from the free South Dakota fold-up, paper road map that they had picked up at the local Standard Oil gas station. Driving on historical ox trails, gravel roads, "two laners," "four laners," and reading the Burma Shave ditch signs, helped to pass the time between sites. The Burma shave signs read like they were lifted right out of a Temperance Union playbook: "Violets are Blue, Roses are Pink, on Graves of those, who Drive and Drink. Burma Shave." Must-see stops included: The Corn Palace in Mitchell, Al's Oasis in Chamberlain, Wall Drug where the water was free and coffee was a nickel, and all the Rapid City area attractions. The highlight of the trip was seeing Mt. Rushmore. When Barbara Rockne and her better half were gazing at Mt. Rushmore, she said, "George Washington looks like he's suffering from an abscessed tooth. Funny they didn't pull it out before he posed."

I Pledge
My Head to Clearer Thinking,
My Heart to Greater Loyalty,
My Hands to Larger Service and
My Health to Better Living . . .

For My Club, My Community and My Country

4-H Clubs can trace their roots back to organizations that were called Corn Clubs and Canning Clubs. By 1911, the four-leaf clover became the 4-H emblem, and by 1912, the name, "4-H Club," became official. To put it in a timeline, the year 1912 was also the year Clara Barton died, the Titanic sank, and great-grandpa Rollef's Mrs. had a spell.

About fifteen years after the Allis Chalmers' tractor made its debut, 4-H Clubs began to sprout up across the landscape like dandelions in a ditch. By the time most farmers had an umbrella in the colors of a field of mustard mounted on their John Deere tractors, 4-H clubs had been established in nearly every township across the nation.

If you grew up in rural America in the '50s, you were most likely a member of a 4-H Club, and like baptism into your family's faith, membership was usually not an option, but a given. Once a month, eight to eighteen-year-old kids who lived in townships across rural America gathered around neighborhood kitchen tables to pledge their heads to clearer thinking, their hearts to greater loyalty, their hands to larger service, their health to better living – and to eat a little lunch. Clubs with names such as Clover Township Country Cousins, Urness Township Eager Beavers, Monroe Township Maidens, Johnson Township Peppy Pals, and Eldorado Willing Helpers, were led by parents and local volunteers. Direction was provided by the County Extension Agents, and unsolicited advice was provided by people like Mrs. Sven Snustad who believed it was her duty to make sure the township youth were committed to their clubs, their community and their country. She once lamented that they should have added another C, the church.

Each individual county had a few of their own 4-H rules which made sense to their members. For instance, the early 4-H Clubs in North Dakota were separated between boys' clubs and girls' clubs. Girls' meetings were held on Saturday afternoon in one of the member's homes. Sometimes they started out with a gathering in the living room for a clarinet solo or reading. They progressed to the kitchen or dining room where lessons and demonstrations took place. Lessons were all about taking care of the home and hearth. Young 4-H kids gave demonstrations called "How I wash my hands," and "How to make a sandwich." Older 4-H kids gave demonstrations on everything from "How to baste darts and turkeys" to "How and why you should sprinkle clothes." Lunch usually consisted of open-face buns or bread covered with ground ham, egg salad or cheese whiz/olive spread, salads such as glorified rice, a variety of home-canned pickles, and dessert of bars or sugar cookies, along with beverages of coffee and lemonade. Boys' clubs met in the kitchen of members' homes in the early evening, after chores and the milking were done. Lessons were about cattle and crops, and demonstrations ran the spectrum from "Getting the most out of your curry comb" to "Controlling blight with DDT." A typical boys' lunch consisted of barbeques, potato chips, pickles, cake and a choice of different types of bottled pop, and coffee for the leaders.

Minnesota clubs followed the rules more than they did in North Dakota when it came to keeping records, and they morphed faster into clubs where town kids were invited to join. Even though social activities such as club softball teams and 4-H Follies' talent contests had nothing to do with crops, cattle or canning, they became embraced, accepted and normalized as being a fundamental part of the 4-H experience. As Mrs. Elmer Stordahl, who always smelled of mothballs, said to Mrs. Nels Lillegaard after they finished watching a 4-H Follies program, "This is just plumb foolishness. What is this world coming to anyway?"

Life continued to change at a faster pace, and about five years before Mrs. Russell Rosholt started writing checks, 4-H Clubs grew their memberships by encompassing more social activities. Even before planting season was over in June, 4-H kids were sent off to camps which offered recreational activities such as swimming, crafting lariats for key chains out of different, colored, plastic strings, greased pig wrestling contests and mud wrestling, if it rained. To make matters worse, the lines between girls' and boys' projects became blurred, and boundaries were being pushed to the limit.

Girls were no longer content to give demonstrations on "How to wash nylons," or sit with other girls on a parade float wearing white blouses, green calico-print, gathered circle skirts, white anklets and black-colored Mary Jane shoes, while embroidering dishtowels under a sign that read, "Don't we seam nice." Girls wanted to shear sheep and show shorthorns. Boys were interested in making seed art, painting pictures of their dogs, and had no issues with modeling gabardine wool suits their sisters had made for them in Make-it-with-Wool projects. Mrs. Elmer Storgaard made known her disdain when she said, "*Uffda,* isn't there any common sense or decency left anymore? Why, five years ago these same boys were proudly standing on a 4-H parade float holding up a sign that read '4-H steers you in the right direction.' They were decently dressed in cowboy boots, cowboy shirts, and clean overalls. Now look at them. They're all slicked up smelling of Lucky Tiger, decked out in a three-piece monkey suit walking on a makeshift banquet table runway in a County Shed Quonset. It looks to me the steers took them down the wrong path. Next thing you know they'll be taking up sewing, and none of them will smell like barn anymore."

State of North Dakota
Trail County

This is to certify that Janet Letnes
                          Eldorado Willing Helpers

has, in this year 1958-1959 , successfully completed the first year of

the 4-H Home Improvement project and is entitled to further privileges and

advancements.

Signed_____
                                    LOCAL LEADER

Anne H. Green
COUNTY EXTENSION AGENT

4-H Achievement Days

Achievement Days were held before the County Fair in the summer for kids who grew up in Minnesota. In North Dakota, Achievement Days were usually held in late September, and 4-H kids were excused from school for two days to show the "goods," and to run around the county sheds and Quonsets that housed the projects.

1957 4-H Project

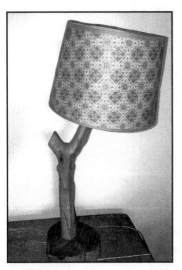

Achievement Days was like a County Fair that was missing a Tilt-a-Whirl, Ferris wheel, cotton candy, carnival games, bingo games, beer gardens and freak shows. Otherwise, they had some similarities. For instance, a person had to pay 50 cents to see the bearded lady at the County Fair, where at Achievement Days it didn't cost anything to stare at Agnes Thorsrud, the Banana and Date Bread judge, whose upper lip hair and chin beard would give anyone the shivers and a run for their money. Looking at the fat lady at a County Fair also cost 50 cents, and at Achievement Days it was free to watch Hilda Storgaard sitting by a table with her body hanging over the sides of her folding chair, smacking her lips as she was tasting a Blonde Betty Bar entry. Ed Johnson, Achievement Days official auctioneer, could easily entice a person to "bid 'em up," and would have held his own if he were put up against a carnival barker who also tried to get people to buy and bid. Also, both the County Fairs and Achievement Days had Lutheran Lunch stands on their grounds where egg coffee, bars, pies, and a host of other things were served.

Winter Shows

Valley City, ND, Crookston, MN, and other cities held events called Winter Shows. They were held at the time of the year when it was too early to get out on the Allis and plant, and there was nothing much to do but taxes and shovel. Winter Shows were a family event where there was something for everyone. 4-H boys showed their livestock and competed in rodeos. Men watched and participated in tractor pulls, and women watched a slicked-up, high-powered salesman trying his best to sell them a new "slicing and dicing knife."

The County Fair

One of the biggest social events of the year was the County Fair. Going to the County Fair was even more exciting than going on a family fishing trip and staying in a cabin on a lake that had "modern housekeeping."

Attending the County Fair was a given for all 4-H kids and their parents. The County Fair timetable and events were pretty much the same year after year. The carnival would come to town and set up on Monday night, Tuesday and Wednesday. Idle town kids – who didn't have jobs or chores and spent their days hanging out at the river or riding their bikes up and down the streets – would watch them set up. Hoods, who lived in town, were sometimes hired to run the rides and enticed to hook up and become a "carnie." A few of them did, but eventually most of them made their way back home.

On Wednesday night, town kids would go to the makeshift Midway to eat cotton candy and ride the Ferris wheel, Octopus and Tilt-a-Whirl. On Wednesday night, country kids would unload their animals in designated stalls, spread the straw, feed their animals and hope for the best.

Bright and early Thursday morning, 4-H kids – who had been cutting the mustard on their entries for at least five days before the fair opened up – came with their projects of popovers, potholders, aprons, gathered skirts, potatoes, wheat, corn, woodworking projects and various other exhibits. After searching through long banquet tables to find the spot where their exhibits were supposed to be placed, and figuring out a "ballpark" time their entries were to be judged, they too hoped for the best.

The women went to their respective church booth lunch stands to cook, serve, sweat and raise funds for their church kitchens. The men went to the barns to look at the animals and watch the judging, and to the machinery buildings to look at the new combines and cultivators before going to the church lunch stands to eat and be served.

Because judging and showmanship competitions would be finished by late Friday afternoon, the country 4-H kids were free to hit the Midway on Friday night. The Midway was lit up, the music was loud and kids were drawn to it like bees to nectar. A caravan of colorful characters lured them into freak shows, talked them into throwing nickels on plates to win a teddy bear, and testing their marksmanship abilities by shooting at plastic ducks. They bought tickets to ride the rides that were run by dirty, unshaven, greasy-haired men with dragon tattoos who had tobacco-stained, rotted-out little teeth, a Lucky Strike hanging out of the corner of their mouths, and visible knife scar marks on their faces. Invariably some girls would throw up after riding the Tilt-a-Whirl, and some got dizzy and fell down in the puke-soaked dirt. Kids drank overpriced bottles of pop, and ate bags of dry-tasting popcorn and lots of pink-colored cotton candy. Many boys remember smoking their first cigarette behind a building or barn.

By Saturday, reality had hit and the verdicts of the judges were made public. Everybody suspected that any kid who received a grand or reserved champion had parents who did everything, except their own name on the project. It was also assumed that the blue ribbon winners had more than a fair amount of parental guidance, too. Those that received a red ribbon usually did the majority of the work themselves, but no one was 100 percent positive about it. It was a given that those who received a white ribbon were on their own. As Edna Bjornstad said to her son, Jerry, who was disappointed that he received a white ribbon on his BB gun rack project, "Well, it's a good lesson. What did you expect when you had to hang your project out the pickup window on the way to the fair to try to get the varnish to dry?"

By the end of the week, the Mrs. was all tuckered out from the heat and the nonstop cooking and serving at the Ladies Aid lunch stand. She couldn't wait to get back home to a normal routine. The Mr. was getting antsy, and all the idle chatter and loud noises were getting on his nerves.

The kids were anxious to get their premium checks, but were getting ready to move on. They picked up their ribbons and their entries of popovers that had caved-in, gladiolus flower arrangements that had wilted, and gathered skirts that would never be worn. The livestock the kids had raised and shown were auctioned off, hauled off, ready for the butcher and became nothing but a memory. Early Monday morning, the carnival packed up and moved out. The fairgrounds, buildings and barns were hosed down and cleaned up. The gates were closed and locked for another year, and the only thing that lingered was the smell of barn.

The State Fair

To kids who got to go to the State Fair, everything seemed bigger, brighter and better – and noisier than a pickup that had lost its muffler. It was filled with women who had earrings bigger than their short-shorts, carnival ride operators who looked like they hadn't eaten in months, and people swarming all over who didn't look like they had roots in Viking Township or in Norway.

Years ago, rural people only went to the State Fair if someone in the family had won grand or reserved champion on their County Fair entries, they had a "souped up" stock car they were going to race, they had relatives they could stay with who lived in the big city, they lived close enough to the State Fair so they could make it back home in the evening, crowds of people didn't make them nervous, they fulfilled a lifelong dream of visiting Machinery Hill, or if a family had a daughter who was crowned Princess Kay of the Milky Way.

A Good Time was had by Most!

Home, Town and Church Celebrations

If you can't find it at the drugstore, the hardware store or at the Johnson Store, then you really don't need to buy it.

As Norwegian Lutherans, we didn't go hog wild when celebrating special occasions. We preferred to spend our time working. We had gatherings, reunions, events and doings. At home, we celebrated birthdays, the major holidays, and yearly family reunions. We put in extra effort when it came to celebrating milestones such as high school graduations, Confirmations, weddings and silver and golden wedding anniversaries.

In the township, we celebrated with basket socials, necktie socials and other socials. These celebrations were sometimes fundraisers for the rural schools.

In neighboring towns, we celebrated the major holidays and acknowledged jubilees with parades, programs and food. In church, we celebrated Christmas, Easter, New Year's Eve, Confirmations and Jubilees. We gathered and participated in meals and programs for raising funds and for fellowship.

Home Celebrations

Birthdays: You could never count on the weather in October!

1st birthday, October 2, 1946

1st birthday, October 31, 1946

Everyone had a birthday, and in some rural areas, neighbors gathered in the evening to celebrate the event. It didn't matter if someone's birthday party was scheduled on a school night because no one had a prescribed bedtime. Besides, no one ever had a babysitter, so all ages–from babies to infirm grandpas – showed up to "wisit" and eat cake.

On their birthdays, kids got a birthday cake complete with candles, a present and a spanking from each member of the family. (One swat was given for each year.) The birthday kid would also get "a pinch to grow an inch, a sock to grow a block and a slug to grow a rug." Siblings usually left out the phrase, "a smile to grow a mile," because it wasn't easy to smile at someone who was getting extra attention. A kid could usually count on grandma and grandpa showing up with a dollar bill tucked in a card.

Family Reunions

Family reunions were always held on the home farm, and relatives, shirt-tailed relatives, and sometimes visitors from the old country would show up, and eat all day. Family reunions were always potluck picnics where bowls upon bowls of food and gallons upon gallons of coffee were eaten and drunk. The women kept busy dishing up food, shooing flies away from the food table, and bouncing babies on their laps. The men would snooze on the grass after they ate, and sometimes play horseshoes. The kids ran wild playing hide-and-seek, pom-pom-pull-away, anti-I-over and other games. Young boys would sneak behind the barn to smoke, some of them for the first time. Kids would climb up and fall out of trees, and jump in lakes and rivers that were located nearby. Usually nobody died at a family reunion, but there were sometimes some close calls.

God Jul

The biggest holiday celebration took place at Christmas time. Preparations took a month, and included cleaning, butchering, baking *lefse* and boxfuls of cookies, getting the *lutefisk*

ready, sewing or buying Christmas clothes, and putting up and decorating a tree with tinsel, gaudy garlands and a few haphazard decorations. Norwegian Lutherans usually celebrated on Christmas Eve. The women served the food on their fancy dishes, and the homes were filled with relatives. Gifts that had been bought at the hardware store, the drug store or the Johnsons Store, were opened on Christmas Eve after the dishes were done.

Easter

Home preparations for Easter included cleaning the house, setting the table with the good dishes, washing the car and polishing the shoes. After church services, ham and a bunch of other stuff was served to relatives. We counted our blessings, but not out loud. The kids looked for their Easter baskets which were hidden all over the house. They contained a few jelly beans and hard, colorful egg-shaped candy with white filling, but no toys.

Thanksgiving

On Thanksgiving Day, we gathered together with too many relatives (in too small of a house) to stuff ourselves with too much turkey, dressing and pumpkin pie. The adults were squished in at the dining room table, and those that were confirmed sat at the kitchen table. The younger ones sat and ate on a stair step, a card table, a blanket on the kitchen floor or any other place they could find to sit. Sometimes the roads were pretty icy on Thanksgiving, and a few had to be pulled out of the ditch.

The only place left for Jackie Bjornstad to sit and eat her Thanksgiving Dinner at the Grimsrud home was in the bath tub. It was in 1959, the year before she was Confirmed. She was a good sport about it.

Valentine's Day: Celebrating love Norwegian-Lutheran style

Celebrating love was an awkward thing for a Norwegian-Lutheran to do, that's for sure. Sometimes on Valentine's Day the Mr. bought a yellow-colored Whitman's Sampler box of candy at the drug store for the Mrs., but everyone knew it was to be shared with the whole family. Everyone wanted to eat the candy with the nuts in them, and by the end of two days, all that was left were a few pieces of dark chocolate that were squished so badly that the pink and white fillings had squirted out all over.

May Day

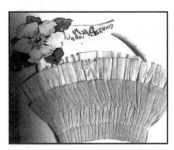

On the first of May, people sometimes would make May Day baskets filled with small flowers, peanuts and chocolate and hang them neighbors' doorknobs. They would take off before anyone saw them do it. The kids enjoyed getting the candy, but no kid ever chased down another one to give them a kiss for it. May Day baskets were squished and glued into scrapbooks and saved for time and all eternity.

Fourth of July

Home celebrations on the fourth of July included picnic food with relatives and the lighting of a few fireworks such as sparklers and black cats. Caps that were pounded with a hammer on the pavement or put in cap guns provided hours of entertainment for kids.

Labor Day

Labor Day wasn't celebrated. It was just something we did six days a week for 52 weeks, year after year after year. Labor brought us satisfaction and basically,

All I Do is Work!

we enjoyed it. We didn't know any better because it was in our DNA, and you can't change that. We never talked about working hard; it was just something we did without complaining.

Halloween

Halloween was celebrated by young kids begging for candy at neighbors' homes. Since nobody had a doorbell to ring, we just opened the door and yelled, "Trick or treat, money or eats." We never got any money, but we were treated with either homemade or "bougten" candy, caramel apples or popcorn balls. Costumes were homemade and weren't fancy. Ghosts were made from white worn-out sheets, and witch costumes were made by dyeing white worn-out sheets black. Many kids wore hobo and gypsy costumes. They were basically a haphazard collection of worn-out clothes. Older boys celebrated Halloween by tipping outhouses, putting chickens in mailboxes and letting cows out.

Grownups didn't celebrate Halloween, but they dressed up in costumes when they went *Julebukking* (Christmas Fooling) to create some fun after Christmas. They also dressed up incognito when they had a mock serenade called a Shivaree *(charivari)* for a newly married couple. Neighbors would go dressed in funny, bizarre "get-ups" to the newlyweds' home in the late, late evening. They would bang on pots and pans and create all kinds of mayhem until they woke the couple up, and were invited into their home for lunch. This certainly wasn't typical Norwegian Lutheran behavior. It was something to do before TV got popular.

Town Celebrations and Remembrances
Fourth of July

Rural folks went to town to celebrate both the Fourth of July and Decoration Day. These celebrations included parades, picnics, programs and politicians begging for votes. Parades, led by local grand marshals that were sometimes self-appointed, were a collection of color guards with flags, gold star mothers, various queens with their courts in convertibles, school bands with students in hot itchy wool uniforms led by baton-twirling majorettes, polka bands by German immigrants, tractors, police cars, fire trucks, and a hodgepodge of crepe paper floats created

151

by various organizations and clubs. The Fourth of July celebration usually ended with a small fireworks display.

Decoration Day (Memorial Day)

On Decoration Day, people would make sure their familys' graves were cleaned up and planted with geraniums. The veterans would be in full uniform, the bugle and taps players would have made sure their spit valves were cleaned, and the ladies of the VFW and American Legion would be peddling plastic poppies.

Every Decoration Day program had a speaker who spoke about sacrifice and freedom, and a young person who read "In Flanders Fields the poppies blow, between the crosses row by row." The band played not only patriotic hymns such as "God Bless America," "The Battle Hymn of the Republic" and "The Star Spangled Banner," but also military hymns such as "Anchors Aweigh," and "From the Halls of Montezuma, to the Shores of Tripoli." There was a lot of saluting and hands over the hearts manifestations on Decoration Day.

Armistice Day (Veterans Day)

Armistice Day celebrations that took place on November 11th were mostly celebrated by veterans and their organizations. These celebrations were usually held at local American Legion and VFW Halls, and involved reminiscing, food and beverages that weren't served in the Lutheran Church. Veterans didn't dance on Armistice Day, but they did rent out their halls to Catholics for wedding dances. It was sometimes difficult for farmers to make it to the celebration because they either had to try "beat the clock" and get the corn finished before the weather changed, or they were hunting.

John Deere Day

John Deere Day wasn't really a town celebration, but rather an event where both town and country people showed up, watched a little partisan movie about the "Green vs. the Red," ate free pancakes and registered for door prizes. Not to be outdone, the International Harvester dealers copied the

John Deere folks and had their own event called, "If it ain't red, park it in the shed." Some of the dealers upped the ante and served sausages with their pancakes.

One day, Mrs. Henry Norgaard, the wife of the Allis Chalmers Implement dealer who kept his books, said to Henry, "We might be a small dealership compared to the big boys around here, but that doesn't mean we have to roll over and play dead. Next year we are going to take the bull by its horns and go whole hog and have an Allis Day. We are going to schedule it a month earlier than John Deere Day and International Harvester Day. 'Yessiree Bob', we are going to plaster the yard and the show room with our orange tractors, and along with pancakes and sausages, we are going to offer them some free orange juice to boot." She never got mad, just even.

Saturday Night

On Saturday summer evenings, everyone – including town people (but not the pastors) – gathered on main street and painted the town red in a modest way.[1] Parents "traded," banked and visited. Women and children often went to town with curlers in their hair. Spinsters, who smelled of lilac water and Lady Esther powder, sat in a car and did their best to get a glimpse of the sinners in the pool hall, and of anyone else who looked like they were three sheets to the wind. Old men sat on benches and reminisced about the war, the weather and other timely topics. Kids tore up and down main street and dark alleys, and bought penny candy and sherbet push-ups that cost a nickel. Some towns even had movies projected on the side of a building as a way to contain the kids. After the winner of the drawing was announced, respectable people went home.

---

[1]Going to town on Saturday nights became a ritual about the time most women became confident enough to navigate "four on the floor." Before that time, immigrants would sometimes clean up on Saturday night and go to a neighbor's home to listen to someone play the accordion or fiddle. People quit going to town on Saturday nights after the television took over their living rooms. They preferred to stay home to watch Lawrence Welk and his dancing champagne bubbles and ladies, and to watch boxing live from Madison Square Garden in New York.

Church Celebrations and Doings
The Sunday School Christmas Program

The annual Sunday School Christmas Program was the highlight of the year for little Lutherans and their proud parents. Preparations started after Reformation Sunday, when opening exercise was taken up with learning one new Christmas song, and the second and third verses to familiar ones. The "pieces" the children had to memorize were sent home after Thanksgiving. The nativity characters, which consisted of Mary, Joseph, angels, three wise men and a few shepherds, were chosen and set in stone. When the day arrived, the children were dressed in their Christmas finery, and after the program was finished they were treated to a bag of ribbon candy, peanuts, chocolate haystack drops and an apple. The ribbon candy stuck to the peanut shells, and the chocolate haystack drops smeared up the new Christmas dresses. There was no lunch served after the Christmas program. Everyone was hoping and praying they wouldn't slide in the ditch with their good clothes on.

The *Lutefisk* Supper

If Scandinavian Lutherans could acknowledge a feast day on the church calendar, it would be the feast of fish, and flatbread, or as it would be called in Norwegian, *En festlig middag av fisk og flatbrød*. Unlike the Catholics who had to eat fish every Friday, Scandinavian Lutherans were only morally obligated to eat it once a year at the annual *Lutefisk* Supper. The supper and all of its trimmings, trappings, committee assignments, and preparations followed the very same order whether it was at *Nordland* or *Trefoldighet* Lutheran. The meal usually began somewhere between 4:00 and 4:30 p.m. and was served until 8:30 p.m. to accommodate those who milked. Everyone was ushered to the pews to sit, reflect, worry about the weather and roads, and

𝕷utefisk 𝕯inner for 1200
600 pounds of *lutefisk*
400 pounds of meatballs
116 pounds of butter
600 pounds of potatoes
276 cans of corn
40 gallons of cold slaw
40 quarts of dill pickles
20 quarts of beet pickles
600 pieces of *flatbrød*
2000 pieces of *lefse*
20 loaves of rye bread (for the Swedes)
60 dozen buns
3500 cups of coffee
Between 5000-6000 Scandinavian cookies such as *krumkake*, spritz, etc.
Vær så god!*
Recipe taken from Second Helpings of Cream and Bread by Janet Letnes Martin and Allen Todnem. Redbird Productions, 1986.

wait for their number to be called before they were herded down to the basement to feast on the *lutefisk, flatbrød, lefse* and the other food that almost seemed sanctified.

The Mission Festival

The Mission Festival took place sometime in the fall of the year and was not a celebration. It was an event that revolved around talks from missionaries home on furlough, slide shows, saving heathens, and the singing of "Lost in the Night Do the Heathens Yet Languish," "From Greenland's Icy Mountains" and "I Love to Tell the Story." A good lunch was served, and kids got to try play the Congo Bongo drums and look at other artifacts they had never seen.

The Harvest Festival

There were two types of Harvest Festivals in Viking Township, and both were done to raise much-needed funds to make up for the dip in summer collections. *Nordland* Lutheran, pulling out all stops and firing up on all cylinders, turned their basement fundraiser into a thinly-veiled Lutheran carnival. They set up cakewalks and fish ponds,

hawked hand-crocheted potholders and "Monday, Tuesday..."
hand-embroidered dishtowels. Chicken, meatballs, corn,
mashed potatoes and gravy complete with buns, pickles
and apple pie made from windfalls was served. The dinner
was a freewill offering, and the women crossed their fingers
instead of praying that they would make some much-needed
money. Gertrude Stensrud left *Nordland* Lutheran because
of what went on at its Harvest Festival. She said to Millie
Hendahl, "They call themselves Lutheran, but they have no
shame. If the good Lord was on this earth, He would walk
right in and overturn their tables." She joined *Trefoldighet*
Lutheran, even though her people were *Halling*, not *Vest-Agder*.

Trefoldighet Lutherans, the *Vest-Agder* people with
Haugean leanings, had put in their charter constitution

that basement selling would be forbidden. However, they still pulled off a Harvest Festival and took in much needed *penger.* They always used the theme "Harvest of Blessings," served ham and all the trimming, and had the pastor challenge those who had been blessed with a good crop to give until it hurt. Usually this piling on of Lutheran guilt worked, but there were some who just ate their ham, put in their dollar, and went home.

New Year's Eve

New Year's Eve wasn't a celebration, but an event. For adults, it was a solemn occasion where members sat silently in the sanctuary, prayed, waited, watched and sang "Wake, Awake for Night is Flying." The service was similar to a funeral. The Luther Leaguers drank cocoa and played games in the basement. The highlight for the youth happened when Willy Bolstad, the janitor, let the kids toll the church bells and ring in the New Year.

Church Doings

The mother-daughter banquet and the father-son banquet, were actually ways to honor parents, and the kids participated by giving the readings and playing and singing the musical selections. Banquets to honor Confirmands and high school graduates took place every year. It was kind of a send-off, letting the kids know they had made it, but also it was a warning to let them know their work wasn't done.

They Spread the Word and some of it was Manure

Even though people in Fish County were a little isolated, they didn't live in a vacuum. They heard the world news, the US news, the news from greater Minnesota and the local news on their radios. In the late '50s, some received more news, thanks to their television sets.

They read about what was going on in the world in newspapers, magazines and letters that they received from relatives in the old countries. In addition to Dougie Johnson, news around Fish County and Viking Township was spread by Earl on Rural Route One, Tillie Torkelson, Mrs. Snustad and rubberneckers.

Earl on Rural Route One

Earl was drafted into the army in July of '42. After boot camp he was sent over to Europe to fight in the big one. He was assigned to study communications, and when he arrived overseas, he was given the job of delivering the letters from home to the troops on the frontline. A couple of weeks before he was sent off to boot camp, he had married a girl from Viking Township who he had only known for a couple of months. She was nine years younger than him, but promised to wait for him. They took the plunge, and said "I Do." Her mother said to her, "Ya, you might not know him too well, but we know of his family, and they're all decent. You just have to make the best of it and it will all work out." While he was gone, his bride inherited a small house on the outskirts of town that belonged to her spinster great-aunt, Lena. She got all the furniture to boot! Her mother reminded her of her good fortune and said, "The Lord provides." Her mother was right.

Three years later, Earl was back in Viking Township with a missing left eye and missing teeth, but all his limbs and marbles were intact. He knew he was lucky. However, he had to give up his dream of taking over the homeplace from his dad. He knew all the blowing dust and whirling barley chaff would create havoc with his missing eye. Earl knew he had to shift gears, but he was one that always rolled with the punches.

Shortly after Earl returned home, he heard there was a job opening up delivering mail on Rural Route One in Viking Township, his old stomping grounds. He went into the Post Office, filled out a little application and met with the Postmaster. He said, "If I can deliver mail to the boys in the trenches of Normandy with bullets flying over my head, I am certainly capable of delivering mail on Rural Route One to the people I know who are mostly my relatives. I even know the names of their dogs." Earl got the job.

Earl took to his job, like a duck did to water. One day he said to his wife, "Sometimes I feel like I'm living the Life of Riley. I don't have any milking to tie me down, any machinery to repair and no fields to plow. I almost feel guilty getting home at 5:00 p.m. It sure didn't take me long to get used to bankers' hours, that's for sure." Nobody was more dedicated to his job than Earl. He was the first one at the Post Office every morning to help sort the mail, and he was the first carrier to have his vehicle loaded and ready to go. If he felt under the weather, he still went on his route. The only times the mail didn't go through was when the snow was coming down so hard and blowing so bad he couldn't tell the ditch from the road. When people received letters from the old country, Earl always hand-delivered them to their doorsteps. He knew firsthand from delivering mail to the boys in the trenches what these letters meant.

The people of Viking Township knew that Earl would not only always greet them with a respectable index finger wave when he passed them, but he would always go above and beyond the call of duty when needed. Many times he helped to herd cattle back into pastures when they were lose, he pulled cars and pickups out of ditches, and carried dogs from ditches that were caught in gopher traps back to their homes. Once, when bachelor farmer Flop Jacobson was passed out cold on the side of the ditch, Earl hoisted him up by his suspenders, threw him in his car, brought him home and plunked him down on the studio couch. Flop, who was married to the bottle, didn't even wake up. Earl didn't wait to see if he would, because the house smelled barn so bad that Earl's glass eye started to water.

Earl always went the extra mile and hand-delivered the mail right to the doors of the widows who had a tough time walking because of bad hips and phlebitis. More than once, he carried Mrs. Thelma Odegaard's garbage out to the burning barrel, and emptied her slop pail down by the river bank. Once, he even delivered a jar of rhubarb sauce to her sister, Pearl, who was also on Rural Route One just down the road a piece, and doing poorly. However, when Mrs. Thelma Odegaard started asking him to deliver unstamped birthday cards to her friends on the route, he gently let her know that would breaking the law. She took it all in stride and said, "Ya, you're right. Maybe I was thinking you were my own personal carrier pigeon."

Earl enjoyed his work, and most of his days were normal, typical and routine. He kept busy filling mailboxes with tax statements in January, seed catalogs in February, farm

magazines monthly, the "Fish County Weekly" on Thursday
etc. There were only six times a year he dreaded the
work. They were: the spring and fall days he had to load
up and deliver the heavy Montgomery Wards and Sears
and Roebuck catalogs, the day after Halloween when kids
played their usual tricks and put either live chickens or dead
squirrels in some mailboxes, and the day the baby chicks,
which had been sent through the U.S. mail, had to be
delivered.

One spring day when the chicks arrived at the Post Office,
Earl knew he had his work cut out for him. He loaded crates
upon crates of the chirping little chicks into his car, and
started on his delivery route. When he finally got to the
Johnson's house, which was his last chick delivery of the
day, Arlys Johnson invited him in for a cup of coffee. He was
so pooped out he took her up on it. Dougie was so excited to
see all the little chicks that he started jumping all over and
flapping his arms like they were wings.

Earl's nose and glass eye had been running all day
from the stuff in the air that came from the loose chicken
feathers. As soon as he took a gulp of the hot coffee, he
sneezed hard. His glass eye popped out and rolled across
the table like a loose marble, and it landed on the linoleum
floor. He sneezed again, and before one could say Jack
Robinson, is upper plate flew out and landed in his coffee
cup. By the time he had picked his teeth up out of the coffee
and put them back in, Dougie Johnson had already picked
up his glass eye. He handed it to Earl and said, "Wow, that's
a big cat eye." Earl chuckled, put his eye back in, took out
his black eye patch from his pocket and put it on over his
glass eye. Dougie said, "Don't let the chickens see you; they
might think you are a pirate."

Earl had a lot of respect for the people on his route. He
knew which folks might be in trouble because they were
receiving official-looking, one-of-a-kind letters from the
sheriff's department, the U.S. government, or the local

bank. He knew which lonely widows were a little out of touch and subscribed to movie magazines, and he figured out that it was Mrs. Snustad who was sending anonymous letters to people and organizations all over the area. But, he kept it all to himself and never said a word. It was probably why he himself never received a warning letter from Mrs. Snustad, and why he was so trusted and well-liked by all on Rural Route One.

Tille Torkelson

Tillie Torkelson was the columnist who wrote the Viking Township News for the "Fish County Weekly." People always joked and said they learned a lot about themselves by reading her column. The picture to the left was taken when she was interviewing Hedvig Haraldson, a local Viking Township pioneer, who was going to be celebrating his 100th birthday. She asked him how he felt. He shook his head and said, "I feel like I'm 101." It was a tough interview because he was so hard of hearing, but Tillie was patient, and that is why she was a natural at her job.

The Fish County Weekly – June 30th 1955
Viking Township News
By Tillie Torkelson

Mary Sodegaard recently came home from the cities after finishing up nursing school at Fairview in Minneapolis. She accepted a job at St. John's in Fargo. We wish her well.

Last Tuesday evening, the home demonstration sewing project was presented by Mrs. Orlin Grimsrud at the Good Intentions Homemakers' monthly meeting. She presented a lesson on tricks for sewing four different kinds of pockets. The meeting was held at the home of Mrs. Elmer Stordahl. A delicious lunch was served.

Selma Sieverson has reported that there is an albino duckling swimming in Amen Lake. She hopes the hawks and the minks leave it alone. She is following him closely with her new binoculars. The columnist says Amen to that!

A group of Viking County 4-H'ers will leave for camp on Monday morning.

Butch Barsness and Porky Paulson were on their way home from bowling in town last Thursday evening when Porky rolled his pick-up. Butch, who was a passenger, was thrown out of the front windshield. He landed in the ditch, but on his feet. Thankfully, they both escaped with minor cuts and bruises.

Emil Hanson was caught in the hailstorm last week when he was cultivating. He received some gashes on the top of his head that had to be stitched up. He said the hail was bigger than pullet eggs. It flattened about 20 acres of his corn. The damage was spotty throughout the county.

Preparations are underway for the Viking Township potluck picnic to be held at Pioneer Park in town on the 4th of July. Everyone is asked to bring their own gunny sacks for the children's race and their own dishes.

Mr. and Mrs. Johnny Hanson celebrated their 25th wedding anniversary at Trefoldighet Lutheran Church Sunday afternoon. Out of town guests attending were Mr. and Mrs. Iver Moe, Mr. and Mrs. Albert Norby, and Mrs. K.H. Anderson all of Herringdal. Their grandchildren put on the program. A good time was had by all.

Mr. and Mrs. Arne Klemetsrud are the proud parents of a boy born last Tuesday. Mother and son are doing well.

Lund Lutheran Missionary Society will meet Tuesday afternoon to roll bandages for the Leper Colonies. Please bring old clean sheets for ripping.

Services were held at Nordland for Ole Langerud on Wednesday morning. He was a pioneer in this area and was known and respected by all. He had been ill since February.

Mrs. Snustad, Mrs. Thelma Arnegaard and Mrs. Nels Lillegaard enjoyed coffee and doughnuts at the bakery last Monday.

Many from the area attended the wedding of Merle Braaten and Norma Jean Stokke last Saturday night. The wedding was held at Norway Lutheran North of Herringdal. Merle is the son of Harold and Ethel Braaten.

Little Dougie Johnson stepped on a nasty rusty nail and had to be taken into the Dr.'s office to get a tetanus shot.

Due to all the rain and sunshine, a fine crop of chokecherries is reported to be out there for the picking.

Trefoldighet Lutheran Ladies Aid will meet in the basement next Wednesday. Arlys Johnson will give an update on the purchasing of new curtains for the basement.

Rubberneckers

Party lines consisted of six to twelve families who shared the same phone line. On each line there were one or two women who spent their days rubbernecking and would always relay the news to their families and close friends as soon as they heard it. Some of them didn't hear too well and some of them embellished the news, and that caused a lot of rumors and falsehoods to swirl around Viking Township.

Mrs. Snustad

Everyone knew Widow Snustad always had a bone to pick, and that she was never afraid to let the whole township know when she disapproved of something. When things didn't go her way, she took to sending foreboding, anonymous letters. She would take tracts from her church, and she would slip them into envelopes and send them to various people she thought needed to be warned about a variety of sins. She sent unsigned, opinionated letters to all the newspapers in Fish County. She also sent many letters to *Trefoldighet* Lutheran Church where she was a member and to *Nordland* Lutheran where she wasn't a member. One year at the

Trefoldighet Lutheran Church annual meeting, the president of the congregation stood up and said he had received an anonymous letter condemning the buying and selling of goods at the Harvest Festival. He said, "Maybe we best be democratic about this and take a vote." Everyone at the meeting had narrowed the anonymous letter sender down to three widows.

Earl from Rural Route One was at the annual meeting, and he knew, without a doubt, the name of the person who sent the letter. He knew Widow Snustad never put a return address on her letters, and that she always sealed her letters with wax. He also knew he would bring that secret to his grave.

Bums, Beggars and Peddlers

Olaf Nielsen getting ready to try to sell his Fuller Brush products to the women on Rural Route One

It had been a tough, trying week for Hazel Grimsrud. Besides hearing in church that Ole Langerud had passed away, she was knee-deep in work getting ready for the Grimsrud family reunion. Because she and her husband, Johnny, lived on the Grimsrud home place, it was just a given that the annual Grimsrud reunion (which was always held the third Sunday in July) would be held at their farm.

As usual, 75 relatives and about 30 shirt-tailed relatives showed up. However, no one irritated her more than the Bjornstad twins, Eleanor and Emma, who were married to her husband Johnny's twin brothers, Orlin and Odell. True to form, they showed up in their new summer frocks and matching white wedgies. They sat around like they were married to pastors, and neither of them had the sense to get up and help Hazel to keep all their kids in line.

Hazel was relieved when Monday morning rolled around and the family reunion was done for another year. She got up before the roosters started crowing to wash and hang out the clothes. Before the flies got thick, she gathered up a bucketful of leftover watermelon rinds to use for pickle canning. On top of it all, she had to help get her daughter, Gloria Jean, packing and off to 4-H Camp. In the late afternoon as she was carrying in the dried wash from the clothesline, she saw a man stumbling down her road. She knew, without a doubt, it had to be a bum.

Before she could get the screen door open, the bum walked right up to her and asked for some food. He was dirty as a pig, and smelled of hard liquor and pee. She quickly figured out that he either lived at the local flophouse, the poor farm, or he was a hobo who had rolled off the rails.

She put down her clothes basket, told him to stay outside and she would go in the house and get him some food. She grabbed a couple of pieces of fried chicken, and her broom. She went back outside, handed him the chicken and told him he had to leave. He didn't move an inch and immediately began to eat the chicken. She put her broom into action and swished him away in the same way she swished away a cat that was trying to sneak in the house. Finally, he left. She went inside and started to sprinkle her clothes.

As they were eating supper that night she said to Johnny, "Trust me, if it weren't for the Bible verse that admonishes us to show hospitality to strangers because we might be entertaining angels, I would have had no problems sending him down the road empty-handed."

Tuesday morning, Hazel was up before the roosters started crowing to start her ironing. She had no sooner heated up her iron when Johnny came back in the house. He told her the swather had broken down and she needed to get to town to buy some parts. She had no choice. The wheat was ready, and the ironing had to wait.

After wasting an hour in town, she was home with the parts, and once again started up her iron. Hazel really didn't mind ironing because it gave her time to think of all the people that had recently irked her, and time to wonder what Ole's wife would think if Ole's niece, who was PG and living at a home for unwed mothers in the Cities, would show up at the funeral.

Right after Hazel had finished ironing and had folded the three large tablecloths that she had used on the tables at the Grimsrud family reunion, Johnny once again came running into the house to let her know the cows had gotten out and were grazing in a ditch that was north of the pasture. She knew he needed her help to herd them back to the barn so he could fix the fence the cows had broken down on their way to the ditch.

Hazel quickly grabbed a white dishtowel out of the drawer so she had something to wave while herding the cows. On her way out the door, she quickly put on her vulcanized four-bucklers and headed to the pasture. In order to get to the north side of the pasture, she had to climb through a barbed wire fence. She grabbed the top wire with her left hand and held it up as far as she could. She put her left leg through, and while she was bending over trying to plant her right leg in the pasture, she stepped into a cow pie. She slipped, and in the process to get her footing, she dropped the wire and a barb cut her back between her shoulder blades. It smarted and it stung, but Hazel knew the cows came first and she had to keep going.

After the cows were in the barn, Hazel cleaned off her

four-bucklers on the manure scrapper, took them off, and went in the house and into her bedroom. She took off her dress, grabbed her hand mirror off her mahogany vanity, went into the bathroom and put her dress in cold water to soak out the blood stains. She turned around in front of the medicine cabinet mirror, and with her hand mirror she saw that the barbed wire cut had not only bled pretty good, but it was as long and curved as a large, shriveled up string bean.

Hazel soon realized it was easier to herd the cows into the barn than to take care of the cut on her back. First, she wrapped the head of her Fuller Brush bath brush with a soft cloth and reached back to clean off the blood, which at this point, was pretty well dried. Next, she took some gauze, smeared it with Carbo salve and wrapped it around the head of the bath brush. As she was attempting to apply it to the barb wire cut on her back, two of her four fingers on her right hand triggered and she missed the cut she was trying to smear with Carbo salve. Instead, she smeared up her right shoulder blade with the salve. Finally, she took a large towel, wiped off her shoulder, put a clean house dress on and decided it would just have to heal on its own.

After she finished her ironing, she packed noon dinner to bring to Johnny who had fixed the swather and was already out in the north forty swathing the wheat.

When Hazel was driving back home from the fields and pulled into her driveway, she saw an unfamiliar car parked in front of the house. As soon as the short, pudgy, fast-talking man got out of his car and opened his mouth, it occurred to her that he was the same salesman that had just sold Edna Bjornstad a set of Grolier's Encyclopedias last week.

When he opened his car door, all she could see was a busted NESW ball on the dashboard, a coffee-stained tattered map, a squished-down felt hat and a can of Copenhagen snuff on the front seat. The backseat was full of grips, duffle bags and suitcases with missing straps and hinges. There were layers of dust covering everything. Hazel quickly surmised he didn't have a wife to clean up after him because the inside of his car was as dirty as the suit he was wearing.

Hazel – who still had to make a couple of pans of bars for Ole Langerud's funeral and bring Johnny lunch out to the field – was trying to figure out a way to politely send him on his way. When he showed her an 806-paged black doctors' book that he would give her as a bonus for buying a set of encyclopedias, Hazel buckled. She went into the house and got some of her hard-earned egg money so she could buy the set of encyclopedias. She had always wanted a good big doctors' book, and she knew she could justify the purchase by telling Johnny she bought the encyclopedias for their daughter who needed them for school work.

When the fast-talking salesman opened his trunk to get out the books he had just sold her, he had to move a tire-jack, a couple of flat spare tires, and a pair of well-worn and scuffed-up, black-colored Mason shoes. *Uff,* she thought to herself, I think the sting from the cut on my back must have caught me in a weak moment.

On Wednesday, Hazel was getting ready to go to church to play the organ for Ole Langerud's funeral. She had just polished her organ flats and was putting them in her drawstring duck-cloth shoe bag that her daughter had made for her as a 4-H project, when she heard a knock on the door. When she opened it, there stood three women and a baby. The woman with the baby on her hip wasted no time asking Hazel for some milk for her baby. When Hazel went to the refrigerator to pour some milk into a tin cup for the baby, one of the women – who didn't have a baby on her hip – asked her if she had any extra food to share. Hazel was uncomfortable with their begging. She quickly gave them a jar of rhubarb sauce in the hopes that they would leave.

She had no sooner handed them the jar of rhubarb sauce when one of them asked if she could use the bathroom.

Hazel, who was getting annoyed at this point, left with the woman to show her the bathroom, leaving the other woman and the woman with a baby on her hip alone in her kitchen. When the woman came out of the bathroom, the three women and the baby left without even saying thank you.

Hazel, who was becoming unnerved, watched out the window until the three women and the baby left the farmstead. As she was getting ready to leave for church, she quickly realized they had stolen her drawstring shoe bag that held her organ flats. She was sick to her stomach, but was thankful that she kept a spare pair of flats at church.

While she was eating lunch with Edna Bjornstad after Ole Langerud's funeral, she told her what had happened. Edna said, "I've heard stories about these types of beggars and stealers. At least the beggar in the Bible was blind. These people have their eyes wide open and have no problem stealing you blind!"

When Hazel and Johnny returned from Ole's funeral, she got out of her good girdle and sat down at her sewing machine to mend the house dress that she had torn on the barbed wire fence. She had no sooner threaded her machine when Johnny yelled from the kitchen that the Watkins man was in the driveway. Hazel, who was tired and had "had it up to her ears" with everything that had gone on during the week, yelled back at Johnny and said, "Don't let him in the house or you'll never get rid of him. Go outside and tell him we need a bottle of vanilla, and we're good on the orange nectar and Carbo salve this time. Let him know there is nothing more we need."

Hazel was relieved when Thursday finally rolled around and she could get out to her garden to pick, clean, snip and get her string beans ready for canning. She was wishing that Gloria Jean would have been around to help, but she was at 4-H Camp until Friday, and the string beans couldn't wait. It was a miserable day for canning. The sun was hot, the flies were thick and the sweat was rolling down her face. By the end of the day, she was all tuckered out. She was thankful she got it done and no one showed up at her door to bother her.

Hazel was up bright and early Friday morning to start cleaning her house for the week. Gloria Jean would be home from Bible Camp about 3:00 p.m., and she wanted to be done with all the cleaning by the time she had to pick her up. She was thankful she had bought an Electrolux Vacuum Cleaner from another peddler who drove into the farm last year. She was a little bothered by the fact that it was made by a Swedish Company, but she didn't dwell on it.

Right after she cleaned all her mirrors with Glass Wax, another product she had bought from a peddler, she went outside to shake her scatter rugs. As soon as she had finished shaking the rugs, the Fuller Brush man drove into her driveway. He was a regular, and she usually didn't mind him, but she wasn't up to listening to him today, especially not after this week. She immediately met him at his car and told him she had to leave to pick up her daughter and he'd have to come back another day. The inside of his car looked like a portable hardware store filled with every kind of brush, broom and mop for every job imaginable. Edna Bjornstad once said, "Ya, I wouldn't be surprised if he showed up some day with a brush that was guaranteed to brush away sins."

As Hazel was driving to pick up her daughter and was about two miles down the gravel road, she passed the Stanley man. Uff, she thought to herself, I'm glad I'm not home. The good Lord knows I don't need any Aqualon, Glass Wax, furniture polish or any more bums, beggars or peddlers to deal with this week.

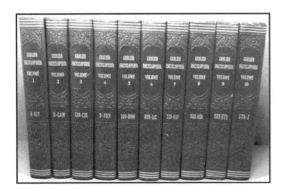

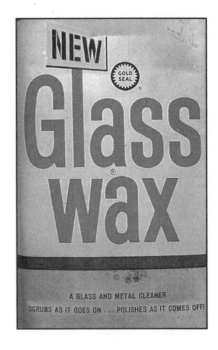

Maladies, Medicine, Measles, Mumps and Mercurochrome

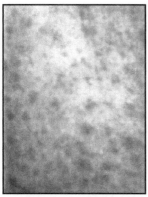

Rubella or Rubeola?

Diagnosing which type of measles kids had contacted was difficult, and came down to guessing. Words describing types of measles sounded like they came out of World War II military playbooks. They were called: German measles, Red measles, Hard measles, Three-Day measles and Seven-Day measles. The only thing we could be assured of was that most kids who came down with measles would itch, cough, develop conjunctivitis and had to be quarantined.

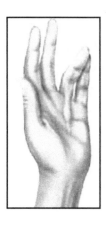

Diseases, Disorders and Debilities

Most of the diseases, disorders and debilities that have plagued us throughout life can either by traced back to our ancestors, or they came from something in the air!

Those of us who have our roots in the Scandinavian countries, and have trouble milking cows because we can't straighten out our fingers, can thank our Viking ancestors for the disease called *Baron Dupuytren*. Hazel Grimsrud, who was the church organist at *Nordland* Lutheran Church for 43 years, finally had to take off her "organ flats" and call it quits when the ring finger on her right hand couldn't straighten up enough to play a B flat. The same disease afflicted her grandmother, Nettie, who had saved her egg money so Hazel would be able to attend Park Region Luther College to learn how to play the organ.

Those of us who were born with "means streaks," are probably related way back to notorious Vikings such as serial murderer, Erik the Red, or his ruthless daughter, Freydid Eiriksdottir.

From the time of the demise of the Black Plague up until the middle of the 19th century, our ancestors were "dying like flies" from contagious diseases like typhoid fever, cholera, diphtheria, dysentery, tuberculosis and smallpox, in addition to dying from war, famine and childbirth.

By the mid-nineteenth century, when our ancestors decided that the grass had to be greener on the other side of the fence, they packed up their trunks and took off to start anew in the hills, valleys and prairies of the Midwest. They had no sooner settled down on their 160-acre homesteads with their kids, cows and crabby spouses, when outbreaks of tuberculosis, polio and the 1918 Spanish Flu epidemic took its toll, in addition to two world wars.

Finally, when vaccinations became readily available for tuberculosis, polio, and DPT, "all seemed quiet on the western front" except for the stock car races in Glyndon, MN, Elvis Presley swaying his hips on the Ed Sullivan show, and the "itis" diseases that periodically popped their heads up and down like Badland prairie dogs.

As youngsters, our "itis" diseases consisted of appendicitis, bronchitis and tonsillitis. As we became older, our "itis" diseases were arthritis, bursitis and phlebitis. Our mothers and our cows fought mastitis, and our pigs and our people fought colitis. Our fevers were Scarlet and Rheumatic, and our rashes were diagnosed as ringworm, measles, mumps, chicken pox and a few puzzling ones.

Diagnosing Diseases from Rabies to Ringworm to Rashes

Back in the '40s and '50s, Edna Bjornstad didn't have the luxury to goggle www.healthdirect.gov. or any other medical site to find out if her kids were coming down with chicken pox, measles, scarlet fever, rabies, ringworm or other mysterious diseases. Telltale signs such as fevers, vomit, diarrhea, rashes and hacking coughs let Edna know that all was not well.

When any of Edna's brood of kids would start complaining about not feeling well, she would instinctively reassure them by saying things like, "Oh, it's probably growing pains," "Oh, you'll live, it will heal," or "Oh, it's just stuff in the air going around." If her kids continued to complain about feeling ill and her daily prayers and their daily doses of cod liver oil weren't "cutting the mustard," Edna basically had five outside sources she could rely on for answers. They were a hunch or notion, the mercury thermometer, the county nurse, her big black doctor book, or – if all else failed and she felt a sense of urgency – she would haul her kids to the doctor's clinic and have him figure it out.

Edna Bjornstad's hunches and notions about what illness her kid had contacted were oftentimes verified by eavesdropping on Mrs. Ole Svensgaard's party line conversations, and by her kids telling her about other kids who couldn't go hunting pocket gophers after school because they were home sick with the same symptoms.

The mercury thermometer was Edna's fact-checking "truth-o-meter" that let her quickly decide if one of her kids was sick enough to stay home from school. When one of her kids complained about "feeling hot," Edna first tested her kid's complaint by putting the backside of her hand on the kid's forehead to see if the complaint warranted getting out the thermometer. If the hand to forehead test proved the complaint might be justifiable, the thermometer was brought out from the medicine cabinet and firmly place either in the kid's armpit or under the tongue to test for a fever. After three minutes, the test results were shown, and Edna made her decision. If the kid's temperature was below 101°, the kid went to school. If the kid's temperature was hovering around 102°, it was a toss-up. Anything above 102° degrees was a win-win for a kid who was hoping to stay home from school.

The county nurse made her rounds once or twice a year to check school children for various conditions and diseases. Many, but certainly not all, county nurses were furloughed post-World War II nurses who were still in full military brigade mode when they signed on to become a county nurse. Many were mean-looking, mean-spirited and mean-acting women who didn't like young children, teachers or their jobs.

The county nurse began school physicals by lining up students like their ancestors were lined up at Ellis Island for their medical examination when they immigrated to the United States. Like their ancestors, the students who passed, could breathe easy, sit down and move on. Those who failed were shamed and sent home.

Basically, the physical consisted of examining a student's eyes, ears, throat, hair and scalp. Anyone who was subject to a county nurse examination knows she took secret delight in pulling ear lobes till they turned red and hurt, gagging students by swabbing both tonsils several times over, and pulling on eyelids till they watered, and the students saw spots in front of their eyes. However, the worst part of the physical was the hair and scalp exam. The county nurse showed no mercy when she put on her gloves and yanked rubberbands out of braids, and dug with her fingernails into "heinie-haired" scalps as if she were pulling angle worms out of clumps of dirt. She checked heads for ringworm, lice, fleas and anything else that seemed to be jumping. If she found ringworm on a student's head, she prescribed the quadruple "Scarlet S" treatments. This treatment involved shaving the hair, skull cap wearing, salve ointment application, and sending the child home till the ringworm cleared up. If the student cried during the examination, they were sent to the corner to stand facing the wall until they quit bawling and shaped up. There were no suckers, stickers or gold stars passed out for not complaining about the examination, or for good health reports.

Edna relied heavily on her 806-paged doctors' book. She got it free, when, in a weak moment, she bought a set of Groliers' Encyclopedia's complete with a ten-volume set of The Books of Knowledge from a fast-talking, traveling peddler who motored into the farmstead one hot, summer day.

Her doctor book became her "go to" Bible when she tried to find out what was ailing her kids. The book not only contained invaluable photos of rashes that would manifest themselves – chicken pox, measles, scarlet fever and ringworm, but also valuable information about prognosis and treatments. Edna's doctor book was also loaded with other common sense and valuable medical information like "How to administer ether," and "How to carefully transport the sick and injured on a homemade stretcher across a rain-swollen ditch."

If Edna's hunches, the county nurse and her trusted doctor book couldn't diagnose her familys' illnesses and diseases, she used common sense. She instinctively knew that if someone in the family had a sustaining fever of 103° degrees or higher, or if she saw things like red streaks going up a leg, it was beyond prayer, patience and perseverance. She had no choice but to motor into town and have her doctor figure it out.

Treatments

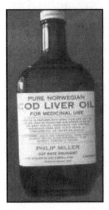

With a brood of kids, and a husband who was no help around the house, Edna knew that containing a contagious disease within the household was as impossible as containing a grass fire on the prairies during the drought years of the '30s. Preventive treatment consisted of vaccinations and booster shots that were administered in the arm, leg or butt, either in the school gymnasium, the hospital or at the doctor's clinic, and daily doses of codl liver oil. (Kids from Wisconsin, who were deficient in salt and iodine, were given goiter pills as a preventive treatment.)

Sometimes it took a "month of Sundays" before all nine of Edna's kids had come down with the same contagious disease and before they were all healed up. At times, it was enough to drive Edna to the edge, and unconsciously she used "The Quarantine" as a passive-aggressive way to say, "You made your bed, now lie in it."

Kids, who were quarantined in their bedrooms, felt like they were locked up in a jail cell. They could only use a "get out of jail" card to go to the bathroom. There was nothing for kids to do but grin and bear it, itch, try to sleep, look at the ceiling, count the dead flies on the light bulb, or study the different patterns in the patchwork calico quilts that covered them.

If preventive treatments didn't work, Edna relied on medicinal concoctions that she made from scratch, bought at the local drug store or ordered from the Montgomery Ward Catalog. Because medicine didn't come with two typed pages of warnings reactions and interactions, Edna just guessed about things like proper dosages and proper usages, and hoped for the best.

Itches were relieved with oatmeal baths and calamine lotion. Vicks Vapor Rub was used for congestions and coughs, and cloves were used for tooth aches. Gargling with salt was the remedy for sore throats. Pepto-Bismol and 7-Up was used for stomach aches and diarrhea, and Milk of Magnesia and the dreaded enema was used for constipation.

 Watkins's Petro-Carbo Salve was the "mother of all salves," and was used for everything from burns, bedsores, bites, blisters, boils, cuts and cracked skin to rashes from ringworm, measles, chickenpox and diaper rash. It was even used on cows as udder cream. It was usually stored in the bathroom, under the kitchen sink, in the barn, and in the cubbyhole of the pickup.

Tinctures

Words such as tinctures, elixirs, potions and liniments that were noted on labels of "boughten" medicines, were as puzzling to Edna's kids as the Biblical words of backbite, beseech, begat, belie and betrothal. The two basic household tinctures, Tincture of Mercurochrome and Tincture of Iodine, were also emblazoned with the cross and skull bone symbol. Seeing these symbols on the tincture bottles, not only gave Edna's kids the heebie-jeebies, but it also warned them that tinctures were not miniature bottles of Watkins's concentrated nectars they could drink.

Sliver, Thorn and Thistle Removal

If a sliver from either wood or metal, or a thorn from a Canadian thistle or cocklebur, buries itself into your finger, the following are common sense ways to remove it.

- Take your two thumb nails and try to pinch and squeeze it out. Pinch it till the skin around it turns red.

- If that doesn't work, put your finger in your mouth and try bite around the area of the skin with the sliver in it.

- If it still won't budge, take out your pocketknife and try cutting around the area.

- If it starts to get red, soak it in Epsom salt, apply a homemade poultice and squeeze some more.

- Ignore it and wait until it starts to fester. Squeeze it again and it might pop out.

- If doesn't pop out by this point, soak it in Epsom salt again and slather it with Watkins Petro-Carbo Salve. Cover it was gauze wrapped with adhesive tape you have cut with your teeth and wait it out for a few days.

- If it starts to get hot, swollen, and streaks start appearing, go to the doctor for a penicillin shot, or you could lose your finger.

Homemade Poultice

Ingredients:

1 tablespoon flour

1 tablespoon mustard seed powder

Water

Directions:

Mix flour and mustard seed powder together in a bowl. Add enough warm water to the mixture to make a thin paste. The paste should be thinner than *rømmegrøt*. It also needs to be of a thicker consistency than the brown gravy that the Sorum boys' served over mashed potatoes and hot beef at their café. They made it daily to serve retired bachelor farmers, town men whose women didn't bother to cook much, and to the men who worked on the railroads and highways. Everybody raved about it.

Application of Poultice:

Get out an old flannel diaper, undershirt or white dishtowel from your rag bag. Any of them will do the job as long as they are clean. Cut two squares from the cloth. Put the poultice on one of the squares, and cover it with the other square. Place it on the area of skin that needs the poultice. Remember, the poultice should not be put directly on the skin or left on for more than 20 minutes. Otherwise, you'll be putting out one fire with another.

Homemade Cough Syrup

Ingredients:
1 ounce of whiskey
1 ounce of honey
1 ounce of concentrated lemon juice
Directions:

Pour the above three ingredients in a pan, stir them a little, and heat up the mixture on the stove. Slowly drink it between coughing fits. (If you're Lutheran, you can substitute the one ounce of whiskey with three ounces of water.) If this doesn't work, rub your chest with Vicks Vapor Rub, cover it with a wool rag and hope for the best. Mrs. Olaf Stensrud said goose grease works just as well as Vicks Vapor Rub, and it's cheaper too. If you're plumb out of Vicks Vapor Rub and goose grease and it's the middle of the night, fill your tea kettle with tap water and heat it on the stove until the tea kettle starts to whistle. Take a white dishtowel, tent it over your head, and bend your head into the steam that is coming out of the tea kettle spout.

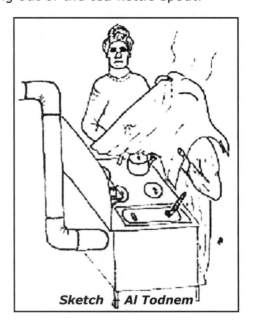

Sketch ‡ Al Todnem

Making Do

Waste Not, Want Not

Back before Fish County put out a county solid waste guide that contained information stating egg cartons are recyclable, but paper plates are a no-no, and before kids had health lessons called "Talking Trans-Fat and the Hidden Dangers of Lard and Mutton Tallow," people just used common sense and lived by the adages —"Use it up, wear it out, make it do, or do without," and "Waste not, want not."

The word "recycling" wasn't in our vocabulary. We used phrases such as, "We can patch that," "It wouldn't take much to fix that," or "We're not throwing that away." We didn't discuss recycling. We just did it, from the slop pail to the string too short to save. The Good Lord told us to take care of the earth, and tend to it by planting shelterbelts. We took Him at his word, except for using a burning barrel.

We didn't expend any energy on how to recycle because everything we owned we used again. Nothing had an expiration date on it. The clothes we made or bought had nine lives. We used rags instead of paper towels, and handkerchiefs instead of Kleenex. Our food came from the ground, barn, lake, woods and sky, and not from cardboard boxes or plastic trays. We put our leftover food in glass or ceramic bowls and covered them with "pantry panties" instead of tinfoil or Tupperware bowls that we could burp. Our beverage containers were glass, not tin or plastic, and our boxes were made from wood crates, not paper.

"Use it up, Wear it out, Make it do or Do Without."

Cloth and Dry Goods

Most clothes we owned were sewn at home and were made with large hems for growing room, and seams large enough to be taken in, and wide enough to be let out. Clothes were made from flour sacks or dry goods. Clothes were passed down, and if they became torn or a moth had created a hole in them, they were repaired and patched. When there was no one left on the "pass down chain," they were put in a box and sent to the mission fields. Socks were darned, and when they were beyond darning, they were saved to be used as rags that could be slathered in goose grease and pinned around necks to loosen phlegm. Old nylon stocking hose with runs in them were made into skull caps, used as Halloween masks, makeshift tourniquets, and filled with mothballs to be hung in a closet.

When clothes were beyond repair and too ragged to send to the mission fields, buttons and zippers were taken off and saved before they were relegated to the rag bag. Good rags became rugs, and rags that couldn't be used for rugs were banished to the grease shed to clean grease guns, and dipped in gasoline to clean off unintended paint splatters. Sheets were ripped into strips to be rolled into balls for bandages and sent off to leper colonies. Any salvageable piece of cloth was saved to be used to make quilt squares.

Food

Bacon grease, lard and fats were put in a tin on the stove and used for frying eggs and potatoes. Potato peel scraps were fed to the pigs, and meat bones and other scraps were fed to the dogs. Egg shells were used as fertilizer for African violets.

Tin cans and Other Metals

Coffee, tuna fish, Karo Syrup, Cream of Mushroom soup, Spam, bandages, Copenhagen *snus* and a few other things were all bought in tin cans. Empty Nash Coffee cans were used for storing cookies made with lard. The smaller, wider Hills Brothers coffee tins were used as water and food dishes for dogs. They were also used for storing skeleton and rusty roller skating keys. Tuna fish cans were used as food containers to feed small kittens before they were old enough to start "mousing." Karo Syrup pails were used as lunch buckets and for gooseberry picking. Cream of Mushroom soup cans were used to store bent nails, on tractor exhausts to keep out moisture, as decorations tied to the back of a newlywed's car, and under the sink as a pee can for little boys. Spam containers and zinc canning lids were placed on window ledges to hold homemade fly poison. Tins that held bandages and Copenhagen *snus* were used to hold miscellaneous small screws, washers and nuts.

Glass Products

Pop, buttermilk, Watkins nectar bottles and canning jars were made of glass. Pop bottles were returned to receive three-cents per bottle reimbursement. Pop bottles that were not returned were used for sprinkling clothes or as a musical instrument for whistling. Watkins nectar bottles were used for homemade maple syrup and for launching fireworks on the Fourth of July. Empty white jars that had contained creamy Mum or Arrid underarm deodorants were used to store snaps and hooks and eyes that had been taken off old clothes. Mercurochrome, Iodine and other tinctures came in glass bottles too. They didn't need to be recycled, because they were never used up or thrown away.

Wood Products

Crates that held lugs of fruit, bushel baskets, wooden spoons, Popsicle sticks and Dixie cup paddles were all made of wood and reused. Crates that held fruit were reused as makeshift cupboards in sheds or playhouses. Cracked wooden spoons were used for spanking and for stirring nectar. Popsicle sticks were used as tongue depressors to check for tonsillitis and other mouth maladies, and Dixie Cup paddles were used to stir small amounts of poultice, and for smearing on underarm Mum or Arrid deodorant cream.

Plastic

Buttons, "boughten" bread bags, breeze bonnets and "pantry panties" were all made of plastic and reused. Buttons were clipped off old clothes, put in a coffee tin and saved until they went on the auction. "Boughten" bread bags

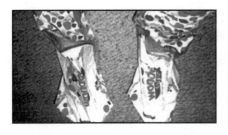

were used to keep shoes and overshoes dry. Breeze bonnets and "pantry panties" were sturdy, and they were either lost or left at church before they were worn out.

Rubber

Old tires became tree swings and beds for petunias. Used rubber hoses were clamped, cut and reused for odd things around the farmstead. Worn out rubber boots and overshoes were used for patching up and vulcanizing various things.

Paper Products

Newspapers, magazines, catalogs and peach wrappings were all reused. After newspapers were read, articles that related to bad weather and personal family events were cut out and sent to relatives who didn't live in the area. Newspapers were also used for covering newly washed and waxed kitchen floors, for wiping down windows and as insulation material.

Magazines were shared with shut-ins, and catalogs and peach papers were used as toilet paper in the outhouse. Christmas paper was ironed and used again, and used envelopes were used for writing grocery lists.

Most people didn't reuse paper from tracts, hymnals, Bibles, Sunday School books, Catechisms and piano books. They fell in the "sacred materials" category.

For Catholics, throwing away "sacred materials" caused guilt and a known participation in a full-knowledge venial sin. This required repentance in a confessional booth, with some Hail Mary's added in for absolution. Lutherans, Methodists, Presbyterians and Baptists also believed throwing away "sacred materials" was a sin, and guilt was sure to follow. They handled it by confessing to God about it privately, and didn't let anyone else in on it. Episcopalians, Congregationalists and Unitarians weren't burdened with any guilt if they threw out scared stuff.

Reducing: It has Nothing to do with Dieting

The present day definition of "reducing" is used in connection to global warming, carbon footprints, the need to "go green" and conservation. Growing up in the '40s and '50s, the word reducing had to do with a woman's effort to lose weight so she could take a deep breath when wearing her "good girdle."

We didn't give a whole lot of thought to global warming and how it impacted the planet. Our world revolved around 160 acres on the prairie, and our landscapes didn't include mountains, oceans or glaciers. Our realities were floods, blizzards or tornadoes. When these things happened, we just left it in God's hands, prayed about it, and cleaned up the mess.

Carbon footprints would be defined in our day as coal dust footprints that Willy Bolstad, the church janitor at *Trefoldighet* Lutheran Church, left on the church basement steps a day after the women had painted them with gray-colored oil paint.

"Go Green," today's battle cry, is a phrase used to educate and encourage us to use natural products. In our day, "Go Green" was a battle cry we yelled to encourage the Otter Falls Otters baseball team to step up to the plate and beat the Herringdal Muskies.

Except for reading about crop rotation and propagation in 4-H, we didn't read books and hear lectures on conservation methods. Leroy Hanson summed up how to conserve heat, electricity and water in three familiar phrases we all heard. "Shut the door, were you born in a barn?" "Turn off the lights, you're wasting good current," and, "We can all use the same bath water."

You Smell Barn!

Fly Poison Recipe: Ingredients and Directions, All in One!

Go down to your fruit cellar and haul up a few of your rusty, zinc canning lids. Mix one tablespoon of formaldehyde and ¼ cup of sugar in ½ pint of water. Fill the lids with the poison mixture. You don't have to wash the lids because the flies don't care, and the object is to drown them. Place them on the window sills, and hope it works. If it doesn't do the job, don't cry over spilled milk because spilled Watkin's nectar on the floor might do the trick. Pour a little concentrated Watkin's Nectar on the floor, and the flies will be drawn to it like a magnet. Once the flies are feasting on the nectar, soak a rag in ether and smother them. If that's

too much work, hang up some sticky fly paper rolls and hope they stick to it. If all of the above methods fail, get out your fly swatter, and have the kids or the retired Mr. start swatting.

We had to use more than elbow grease to get rid of lingering smells of barn. The smell of barn permeated the skin, the clothes, and the air around everyone who came in contact with them. The smell of barn was just one of the smells we tried to rub out and eradicate when cleaning up ourselves and our surroundings. We had smells of dead flies, grime, grease, gasoline and slop pails that we tried to tackle, and sometimes not with a whole lot of luck.

Cleanliness is Next to Godliness!

Sprucing up the Farm

It was no small task to clean a farmstead with all its buildings and grounds, and it took the whole family expending time, effort and sweat to get it done. Like with anything else, most of the work fell on the women. Some of the buildings like Quonsets, Butler bins, storage sheds and granaries were pretty easy to clean. All you needed to do was sweep the floor with a good broom. Nobody bothered to clean cobwebs or windows in these buildings, except for people like Hazel Grimsrud, who was "sorting dust" before

her daughter's Confirmation. A bunkhouse, which was kind of a mini-flop house for transient field workers, was pretty much left as is except for a little sweeping.

Places like blacksmith shops and grease sheds were never cleaned because there was no need to clean up welders, grease guns or grease barrels. You just walked into these buildings, looked around and rearranged things to make it easier to find things. Pump houses were so little that nobody bothered to clean them. Potato warehouses and chicken coops were shoveled out, but never hosed down.

By far, the worst job was the task of cleaning up the milking parlors and the dairy barns, loafing barns, farrowing barns, horse barns and turkey barns. They all smelled barn! Before they were sprayed down with DDT, the manure had to be shoveled into a wheel barrow or front-end loader. Before one could hose the whole place down with water, the hay and straw from the stanchions to the doorways had to be swept out of the barn. It was enough to make anyone, like Norma Jean said, gag a maggot.

Sprucing up the farm also meant burning the ditches in the spring, mowing the lawn in the summer, cutting the big weeds around the buildings, and painting and repairing buildings, fences and anything that looked so bad the Mrs. was ashamed of how shabby they looked.

There were three main occasions that required extra attention for "sprucing up" the farm. They were: a family Confirmation or a daughter's wedding, when shirt-tail relatives from Norway were coming to visit, and when an aerial shot of the farm with the surrounding shelterbelts was going to be taken.

Cleaning up the House

The mundane tasks of cleaning the house were religiously done on a daily and weekly basis. Every task was scheduled

to be tackled and completed on a certain day, and those rules and regulations were set in stone. However, three times a year, in the spring, fall and before Christmas housecleaning took on a whole different meaning.

Spring Cleaning

Sometime between the vernal equinox and Easter, Scandinavian Lutheran women were infected with "Spring Housecleaning Fever," a malady that struck for three to four weeks every spring and was as contagious as chickenpox. During this time, all the stops were pulled out. Everything was turned upside down, inside out, and then put right side up and right side out again. This cleaning also included the outhouse which was considered an extension of the house rather than an outbuilding.

Dishes and silver pieces that were used only for special occasions like silver wedding anniversaries and Confirmations, were taken out of storage, washed, polished, and put right back where they came from. Old shelf paper was discarded, and new was put in place. Deep freezers and refrigerators were defrosted, fruit cellars were cleaned, and any jars of canned food that had bulging lids were thrown. Kitchen tables with leaves in them were pulled apart, and a knife was used to scrap the gunk off where they were joined.

Pillows were taken off davenports and chairs and vacuumed. Vacuum cleaner attachments were used to clean out the insides of the upholstered furniture. Curtain and doilies were washed, pressed, stretched and starched.

Mattresses were flipped, and sprung coils were fixed. Blankets and quilts were hung out to freshen up, and pillows were aired out. If pillows needed re-ticking, they were re-ticked. If someone in the house died in bed, all bedding was washed.

Winter clothes were cleared out of closets, out of the drawers, and shaken out, hung out, brought back in, put in mothballs and laid to rest until fall. Rugs were whisked off the floor, put on the clothes line, and were beaten to death with a beater.

Walls and ceilings were scrubbed, windows were washed and storm windows were taken off, hosed down and put away until fall. Screens were put on, and any hole in a screen was repaired. Light fixtures and window ledges were cleaned of dead flies. Absolutely nothing was left untouched. After all the work was done, the malady subsided, and everything returned to normal.

Fall Housecleaning

After the harvest was in, the canning was done, and the church fall festival was over, "Fall Housecleaning Syndrome" set in. Every type of housecleaning that was done in the spring was repeated in the fall, and done in reverse.

Jeg er så glad Cleaning

Pre-Yule cleaning wasn't as intense as spring and fall housecleaning, because it was so dark at that time of the year nobody could see what you had cleaned anyway. Besides, the time was taken up with baking, *lutefisk* suppers and Sunday School Christmas Program practices.

Cleaning Up the Church

The church also was cleaned really good twice a year, once in the spring and once in the fall. The men took care of the grounds, except the women weeded, planted the flowers, washed the windows and tombstones, and cleaned the outhouses. Basically, the men mowed, shored up anything that was busted, and put oil on the gravel road. The women did all the cleaning inside of the church, and that ran the gamut from cleaning and varnishing pews

195

to painting inside basement steps to cleaning everything in the kitchen and the adjacent basement room where they ate lunch, held banquets, and held Sunday School. All the women of the Ladies Aid came to help, and if they didn't show up, they knew they needed a good excuse. The older ones, who were getting up there and couldn't bend or get around too well, sat and refilled the tract rack, and dusted the hymnals and books.

Some churches had parsonages, and some congregations asked their members clean the parsonages twice a year. People expected the pastor's wife to keep up with daily chores, but they felt obligated to go in and help her with the "big stuff." Most of the pastors' wives were grateful for the help, and pitched in and worked right along with everybody who was working. But there were some like Pastor A.I. Torstensen's wife, Elizabeth Gunhild, who was a perfectionist but wouldn't lift a finger to help. She just walked around her house when the women were cleaning and made sure they did it exactly the way she wanted it done. If she didn't think the job they were doing was good enough, she would try to guilt them by saying something like, "You know Pastor can get fussy about thing. I know he would like it done this way."

Once after Emogene Flestrud and Shirley Solsgaard had finished cleaning the parsonage and were getting in Emogene's car with their buckets, mops and rags in hand to go home, Emogene said, "Well I'll be, can you believe she had me wiping down the inside of the covers of her spice tins, and then she had the nerve to ask me to rewipe the nutmeg tin again because she saw a couple of specks left on the inside cover. With her cataracts, how could she even see them?" Shirley replied, "My Orlin always says, Sometimes even a blind squirrel finds a nut now and then."

Cleaning up the Body which didn't include the Soul

Even though the phrase "Cleanliness is next to Godliness" wasn't in the Bible, we connected it because we took our baths on Saturday night so we would be clean for Sunday services. We left the soul cleansing up to the pastor who tried his best during Sunday services.

Saturday night baths were a weekly ritual for the whole family. They were either taken in a galvanized tub out on the lawn in the summer, or in the house by the cookstove in the winter. The tub was filled with water once, and everybody from oldest to youngest used the same water. By the time the youngest one was bathed, it was more like a "dip and lift" due to all the sediment in the bottom of the tub.

As the years went by, lucky people had a cast iron tub installed in their bathroom for bathing. The elderly, who were too old or infirm to jump in a tub and had to rely on a bowl and pitcher to take a "sponge bath," were the unlucky ones. A few farm homes had showers in their basement for the men to clean up after doing chores, but they were for men only. Also, if push came to shove, some bachelor farmers just jumped in the stocktank or a lake to clean up and to get rid of barley itch.

Daily cleaning up was done before meals by washing the face and hands in a sink or bowl with soap and water. Necks and arms were washed by men who had dirt creases in the neck and elbow bends from field dirt. "Spit baths" were given to boys by their mothers who noticed right before they were going to enter into church that they still had dirt in their ears or on their neck.

Cleaning up products for Women

Bar soaps with names such as Camay, Palmolive and Ivory were used by women when tub bathing. After they had cleaned up, most women moisturized their bodies with lotion such as Jergens, which smelled like almonds. They topped it off with a healthy sprinkling of Cashmere Bouquet Talcum powder to help contain sweat.

Grooming products for Men

Most men had more grooming products for their horses then for themselves. Young boys with heinie haircuts, and old men who were bald, didn't need shampoo. Men who did have hair, just shampooed with bar soup. Men who had butch haircuts or Elvis Presley slicked-back ducktail cuts, used Wildroot Cream or a pinkish-colored butch hair wax to tame down crew cuts, butch cuts and ducktails.

Boys started shaving about the time they were Confirmed, and usually received a shaving kit as a Confirmation gift. When they were older, and both their bodies and beards were heavier, they lathered up with Burma-Shave or Barbasol shaving cream before shaving with their handheld Schick razors and splashed on Mennen Skin Bracer when they were done. Every time Olaf Stensrud put a new blade in his Schick razor, he would nick himself on his neck. To stop the bleeding, he would wad up a tiny bit of toilet paper and place it on the nick. More than once, he walked into

Trefoldighet Lutheran church with the toilet paper still intact on his neck.

Young men who were out to attract young ladies would splash on Lucky Tiger or English Leather Cologne after a shave.

All you need is Lard, Lye and Rainwater!

Homemade soap

Ingredients:
8 pounds of lard
17.6 ounces of lye
28 ounces of rain water
Directions:
Heat the rain water and add the lye. When all the lye is dissolved into the water, pour in the lard! Make sure the hot mixture doesn't splash on you because if it does, you'll have some burn to deal with. After the soap has cooled, pour the mixture into a mold. (You can use old, rusty jelly roll or cake pans for molds.) When cool, cut the hardened soap into bars. Tell the kids these bars aren't for eating. If they sass back or are heard saying words like "H-E-double toothpicks," give them a mouthful.

"Warshing"

Farm women from the Midwest washed clothes every Monday morning unless they were giving birth, or someone in the family had died. When farm women first came to the prairie and set up housekeeping, washing clothes involved hauling water, heating water, and scrubbing dirty clothes by hand using only a washboard that was plunked in a galvanized pail of hot water and homemade soap. No wonder there was a warning written in The Doctor's Book that excessive exertion of scrubbing clothes might lead to a spontaneous abortion.

Wringer washers became a mainstay in most farm homes  long before clothes dryers became a staple. Nobody had a recipe for washing, but everybody did it the same way. After the dirty clothes were sorted and separated into piles, the washing machine tub was filled up with about 20 gallons of hot water. The hot water came from a hose that was connected to the laundry tubs. Soap was added, and the agitator was started.

Directions: Start by washing the white pile first so you don't have to change the water. All you have to do is keep adding a little bit more soap with each load. Agitate the "whites" for about 20 minutes, (barn clothes take about 45 minutes), then wring them out with your hands like you would wring a chicken's neck that you were about to butcher. Next, throw them in a laundry tub for rinsing. Put the second pile of whites in the washing machine tub, and repeat the process until all the loads are done. The rinse water should be diluted with "Mrs. Stewart's Bluing" if you don't want a dingy wash. Now, take the clothes that were wrung out before they were put in a laundry tub for rinsing, but are now water logged, and let the wringer that is attached to the washer wring them out. It will flatten them like a pancake. However, if you get your fingers caught in the wringer, it will flatten them too.

Once Mrs. Einar Jacobson got her hair caught in the wringer. She was nearly 84, still had braids that she wore encircled on the top of her head, and had a bad hip. She should have known better and had her hair pinned up, but she didn't. Unfortunately, she got herself tangled up and in a real mess. She stood bent over from the waist for about 20 minutes unable to untangle her hair from the wringer. It's a good thing Einar came in for lunch, or who knows what would have happened. He was no better. Once he got his shirt sleeve and other body parts caught in the grain auger. He was lucky she was bringing lunch out to him at that time, or he wouldn't have been around to talk about it.

Hanging Out

Heavy duty barn jacket was kept on the line to try to air out the barn smell

We used "solar energy" to dry our clothes in the summer. We hung them out on six metal lines which were attached to two wooden or metal poles that anchored the lines. Clotheslines were located near the house and away from shade trees. During the winter months, our clothes were frozen stiff while hanging on the lines. When we brought them inside, we hung them from door knobs, make shift lines across door lintels, in the basement, on top of radiators, and anyplace we could find that would work to dry them. When we put wet, wool snow pants and mittens on top of a radiator, the steam from the radiator would smell like singed wool, but the moisture helped keep down the static electricity that made our hair stand on end and gave us nasty shocks.

Just as there was a protocol for washing clothes, farm women also followed a protocol when hanging out the laundry. First they carried the wet clothes, an old wet rag, and the clothpin holder bag up from the basement and out to the clothesline poles. They started the "hanging out" process by putting the rag in their right hand and encircled it around line one. Next they reached up over their head and started walking with the rag to clean the lines of dirt, dust and bird droppings. When that was done, the hanging began. Hanging started from the back line which was line six. They did it this way so they wouldn't get all tangled up in the clothes.

Line #1 was the one that could be seen by anyone who drove into the farm, and it was used for sheets. (Women only washed and hung out one sheet per bed because top sheets were rotated to the bottom.) Line #2 was for clothes that were the color of house dresses. Shirts fell in the category and were hung by the tails – not the shoulders. Line #3 was for underwear because no one would be able to see them from the road. Line #4 was for dark clothes, and it was mostly used for men's clothes. Pants were hung by the bottom, and socks were hung by the toes. Line #5 was used for towels and rags. Line #6 was for barn clothes, and they were usually the last articles of clothing to dry.

The sheets were the first to come off the line. Before farm women folded them and put them in the basket, they put their nose in them, closed their eyes and drank in and savored the wonderful smell. It was "poles apart" from the smell of barn, but like the smell of barn, it was a smell nobody ever forgot.

One Cannot Live on Beauty Alone

This is Most Certainly True!

From the time they could reason, Scandinavian Lutheran women were told that "beauty is only skin deep." The word "beauty," and other synonyms of the word, took on a whole different meaning in Viking Township and elsewhere. "She's a beauty," were words used to describe a horse, not a woman. "Good-looking" was often used to describe a slab of *lutefisk*, i.e., "Ya, dat sure is a good-looking piece of fish, den." The word pretty was oftentimes used in conjunction with weather descriptions such as, "The snow on the trees was awfully pretty this morning."

We equated words such as beauty, pretty, cute, gorgeous and handsome with words such as vanity, arrogant, big-headed, lustful and sinful. It was no wonder Scandinavian Lutheran rural folks had a tough time complimenting someone on their physical beauty. If backed into a corner to comment on some person's beauty, it was done in such a way that nobody was embarrassed or felt uneasy. For instance, a person would never just come right out and tell a mother her baby girl was cute. They would expand on it by saying, "Oh my, she's cuter than a button," or, "Why, she's cuter than a bug's ear." No one would just go up to a young girl and tell her she was pretty. A grandma would come close to it when saying, "That dress looks pretty on you." Also, a person wouldn't call a boy handsome. Rather they would comment on "what side he took after," and that depended upon which grandpa was more handsome. Everybody knew without saying what grandpa they were referencing.

"Gussying Up"

Most Scandinavian Lutherans believed that real beauty had to do with being nice, wholesome, pleasant, honest, sensible, sturdy and hardworking. But women were women, and Scandinavian Lutheran women from the farm were no different. They tried to look the best they could with what they were given, but not coming off as being vain.

By '54, advertising with photos and verbiage of beauty products, clothes and patterns started to worm their way into the Farm Journal[1] and other farm magazines that had sections designated for farmers' wives. From Noxzema Cleansing Cream to Henna Hair Dye, to patterns for stout women and photos of young women who had "Made it with Wool," Viking Township women were inundated with convincing ads on how to "gussy up." They were swayed, and they bought. However, they didn't go overboard.

Farm women's beauty products included a pale-colored (Barely Pink or Soft Tangerine) Hazel Bishop lipstick tube and a compact of Lady Esther loose face powder. Blonde or red-headed Scandinavian women used eyebrow pencils for penciling in their invisible eyebrows, because none of them were born with auburn-colored, arched Rita Hayworth eyebrows. Evening in Paris, or Blue Waltz Perfumes were bought and used only for good. Clear nail polish was used for really special occasions like anniversary celebrations or daughters' weddings. (The main purpose of clear nail polish was to stop runs in nylon hose stockings.)

Women on the farm never used rouge because they didn't need it. In the summer the heat turned their cheeks red, in the winter the cold weather turned them red, and in the fall and spring, they just pinched their checks if they needed color.

[1]in '54, the "Farm Journal" was even advertising Hammond Home Organs. One of their advertisers stated that playing the organ would help a person think more clearly. Evelyn Thompson, who was going through the change and some tough times, bought one in hopes it would do the trick. It didn't help much, as her husband ended up sending her away for awhile.

[2]Some of our perfume bottles had labels on them that said *Eau de Toilette* or toilet water, rather than the word perfume. The women in Viking Township could never figure out why. When the Avon Lady started to show up on doorstops, town women bought perfumes from her with enticing names such as Here's My Heart, Topaz and To a Wild Rose.

Homemade Flax Gel for Finger Waves

Ingredients:
1 cup water
1 tablespoon whole flax seeds
1 teaspoon sugar
Directions:
Mix the above three ingredients and bring to a boil. Cover and simmer the mixture for 15 minutes. Strain out the seeds immediately, or they will be impossible to get out. If you don't see well and put this mixture in your hair without straining, you will look like you have little gnats all over your head. That's what happened to Audrey Olson, and everyone at Ladies Aid saw it. She tried to hide it with a hairnet, but she didn't fool anybody. The setting gel will store well for about two weeks. After that, you better throw it in the slop pail.

How to Put On a "Good Girdle"

Directions for putting on a "Good Girdle:"

Open your window and hope for a good strong north wind. If there is no wind to circulate air, turn on a fan at a speed that would make a sticky flypaper strip whirl.

Sit down on your bed and bend forward, but not too far or you might get a little woozy and not be able to finish what you started. *Uffda,* you would really be in a bind, if you know what that means.

Put both legs in the girdle,

pull'er up part way, and then rest a little. Lie down and pull 'er up the rest of the way. This method cuts down on needless squirming. Because a girdle can get so snug that it cuts off air supply, take it easy when sitting up. With a limited amount of air supply, toppling over from a spell could happen. Think what would happen if the pastor or Watkins man walked in and found you crumbled over with just your girdle on. You'd never be the same again.

Putting on a good girdle is mighty hard work. It's as hard as trying to loosen up rusty lug nuts on a tractor wheel. It takes time, patience and strength.

The Kitchen Queens and Other Royalties

Immigrants left the old countries to get some land and to get away from kings, queens, bishops, pastors and priests who thought they had a direct line to heaven. However, it didn't take long before a "royalty infestation" took over on the prairie like Canadian thistles did in a potato field.

Royalty in the church

There were two classes of royalties in the Lutheran and other Protestant churches. One was self-appointed, and one was "crowned;" not in a traditional way, but in a Lutheran way.

The self-appointed queen was usually an outspoken, matriarchal woman who put herself in charge of the kitchen and everything that went with running it her way, and her way only. She made sure she was always the pigeon, and not the statue! When the matriarchal queen was finally laid to rest, there was always another new one waiting in the wings to ascend to the "kitchen throne." There was never a vacancy for this spot.

The "crowned" queen in Lutheran and Protestant circles was a pastor's daughter. At an appropriate age, she was always chosen to play the role of Mary in the Sunday School Christmas Program. If the pastor didn't have a daughter, the Sunday School superintendent's daughter was next in line to play the role. If the Sunday School superintendent didn't have a daughter, the "crowning" went to a girl who was blond and good at memorization – even though nobody could see her blonde hair because it was covered in a Dan River light blue percale sheet, and the girl who played Mary didn't have any speaking parts. It was just a given that if the pastor had a son he would be chosen to play Joseph.

Because priests didn't have daughters, and Catholic kids didn't have Sunday School Christmas programs, there was no "role playing" of Mary in a blue sheet. The Catholics crowned queen was the real Mother Mary. During the month of May, young Catholic girls with flowers in hand and dressed in their First Communion dresses, would parade to a statue of Mother Mary and put a crown of flowers on Mary's head. Lutherans didn't have statues in their churches, so they just made May baskets and handed them out to their friends on the first of May.

Royalty Straight from the Farm

Youth organizations such as 4-H and FFA often elected kings and queens as representatives, but their duties didn't amount to much. They were more or less popularity contests. Farm organizations also had queen competitions, but they weren't popularity contests. Cattlemen queens were "master-milkers," and had to know how to flush out mastitis bugs. Pork queens had to know how to castrate pigs and talk hogs like the big boys. Rodeo queens had to know how to ride, race and barrel jump without having their cowgirl hats fly off. Unlike other queens, farm organization queens didn't have to know how to tap dance, twirl baton or solve world problems. The duties of farm organization queens involved riding in local parades, attending county fairs, state fairs and winter shows.

The farm girl who won Minnesota's Princess Kay of the Milky Way won the "mother of all" farm queen competitions. Not only was she awarded a dozen roses and a scholarship, but more importantly, she had an image of her head sculpted in butter at the Minnesota State Fair. Because she had to pose in a freezing room for six to eight hours while her head was sculpted, this was no easy task. Most queens kept their butter sculpture in the deep freeze until their family butchered and ran out of room to store it.

"Queen for a Day" Royalty

Unstable women, who lived in town and were good at bawling and faking tears, were masters at figuring out a way to be a contestant on the radio and television show, "Queen for a Day." They wanted to be on the show so they could snag a free Speed Queen washer or some other unnecessary thing. These women who liked to draw attention to themselves were not farmer's wives, Norwegians or Lutherans.

Part III
All Things Must Come
To An End

The Rosholt Family

Three generations of Rosholts – Left to right:
Ralph, Halvilde, Rollef, Unknown and Russell

Ralph, the second generation Rosholt, was the tall lanky one. He always looked ten years younger than his age, and didn't look like anyone in the family. Nobody could figure out why he looked the way he did, but they didn't say anything. He is standing by his Grandma Halvilde who was big boned and short. She is standing by her husband, Rollef, the first Rosholt homesteader who is also short, and is hiding his *Alt fra Norge* cane behind his back. We're not sure who the lady is who is standing by Rollef, but we're guessing she's some shirt-tailed relative of Halvilde. Ralph's son, Russell, is standing on the end. This was taken before Russell's wife, Shirley, was in the "picture". Rollef passed on shortly after this photo, but Halvilde lived way up into her '90s, even though she suffered from bouts of phlebitis. We figure Ralph's wife, Olga, must have taken the photo.

The Rosholt Twins –
Judgment Day
at Achievement Days

The Rosholt twins and their competition

It was Thursday, June 7, 1956 when Russell Rosholt and his ten-year old twin boys, Rodney and Roger (Rod and Rog), loaded up their 4-H project pigs, Petunia and Penelope, in the back of the family's '52 blue Dodge pickup and motored into town for the annual 4-H Achievement Days. Russell's Mrs. didn't go along because someone had to stay home to milk, slop the hogs and feed the sheep. Besides, she was knee-deep in canning rhubarb.

The boys were excited because they knew they could

talk their dad into taking them to the local café to get a hamburger, fries and a chocolate malt for noontime dinner. It was the first time they were entering a 4-H project for competition, and they had their hearts set on getting a "blue." Russell was more realistic about the whole situation, but didn't say anything because he didn't want to burst their bubbles. Besides, he had enough on his mind with the news that Eisenhower might run the new highway less than one-quarter of a mile west of his farmstead.

Russell and his wife, Shirley, had helped to start the Viking Victory 4-H Club so the twins could get a handle on what it takes to be a pig and small grain farmer. They were hoping at least one of the twins would have farming in his blood and would decide to be a fourth generation Rosholt farmer on the homestead. Russell was thankful that when he got discharged in '44 from "the big one," he escaped with having just a few minor facial tics, a pesky foot rash, some hearing loss and heart palpitations when he heard loud noises. He was also thankful that a year later, in '45, Shirley Julesgaard,[1] the neighbor girl, said she was willing to set up house for him, and his dad, Ralph,[2] felt it was time to hang up his barn jacket and take a pass on the pigs.

Ralph was just plain lucky he made it home from World War I in one piece. While in the trenches overseas, he was hit by flying shrapnel and just about lost his right leg. He never complained and just did what he had to do to get by in life. He was just thankful that during the '30s he was able to hang onto his dad's homestead given the Depression, the Dust Bowl and the Drought.

In the fall of '46, despite the fact Shirley had suffered her whole life from female issues, they were blessed with twin boys, Rodney and Roger. Rodney was the first one out of the gate, looking like he was doing the *Halling*[3] and bellowing as loud as Old Bossie did when she got her foot caught in a gopher trap out in the pasture. Roger came out a few minutes later, and didn't utter a peep until they realized he had the cord wrapped around his neck. After they got that straightened out, he just whimpered like Blacky, their old dog, did when Shirley took the Howdy Doody puppet out of his mouth that Roger had received from his Grandma Olga when he came down with the chicken pox.

When Grandpa Ralph first saw them, he said, "It's hard to believe they came out of the same liter." Shirley agreed that Grandpa Ralph had hit the nail on its head and replied, "You think I'd popped out Esau and Jacob. Rodney is just like Esau. He's always hunting, shooting pigeons and sparrows off the barn cupola, always trying to get others to do his work, always has chokecherry stains on his shirts, and you can't get him to stay put for love or money. He's just like his dad. He's got ants in his pants. Roger, well, he's like Jacob. He's quiet as a church mouse, keeps his nose to the grindstone, and the pig pen clean. He's good at letting his brother always win at arm wrestling, too. He takes after our side. Who knows? Maybe he's being called to be a Lutheran pastor."

Rodney might have self-appointed himself "king of the castle," but they both knew that Roger was "king of the hog house." When Porky, the family sow, gave birth to a liter of six, there were only two that survived. Russell said, "Well, boys, here's your 4-H projects. See what you can do, then." Rodney named his piglet Petunia, and Roger named his Penelope, but after about a week of working with Petunia, the fun and newness wore off for Rodney. True to form, he lost interest and just assumed Roger would be doing the grunt work for both of them.

By the time Achievement Days rolled around in June of '56, Roger had more than paid his dues. He had worked 100 straight days with the pigs – feeding them, recording their daily intakes, training them, caring for them, and getting them ready for "judgment day." Rodney was just counting on Roger to pull them both through.

The pigs both "took blue," and the boys couldn't have

been more excited. Russell took the boys for noon dinner at the local café, and even let them put a nickel in the jukebox located right at their booth. When the waitress was taking their orders, she yanked up her bra strap which had slid down to her elbow, bent over and said, "Do you boys want milk with that?" Stifling laughter, they said in unison, "No! Chocolate malts." Russell chuckled to himself. The first day everyone hit the jackpot, including the pigs.

All good things come to an end, and day two turned out to be one for the history books for the Rosholt Twins. It was showmanship day, or better yet, judgment day! The stakes were high, and it was Roger's day to strut his stuff. He was well-prepared. Into his dad's World War II tattered looking duffle bag he had carefully packed all the essentials. They included castor oil to shine up Penelope, a scissors and shaver to trim stray hairs, a pig bristle brush, rags for last minute clean-up, a rope, small #2 potatoes for his pocket, his dad's army canteen, and most importantly, his great-grandpa's *Alt fra Norge* hand-whittled cane to be used as his guidance baton.

Roger and Penelope were first out of the gates. Roger weighed 110 pounds, but Penelope weighed 130, so it came down to brains over brawn. The makeshift showmanship ring consisted of a bunch of hay bales stacked up two bales high in a circle that was about 20 times the diameter of cakewalk circles at Clifford, North Dakota High School's annual school carnival. It had rained the night before and the ring was filled with mud, several large puddles, manure and loose straw that the wind had blown off the bales and into the ring. It looked and smelled like a pigsty, but Roger wasn't intimidated. He had practiced for months, and knew he could pull it off. With Penelope by his side, he guided her into the circle carefully steering her away from the mud and manure piles while gently nudging her under her chin with his great-grandpa's *Alt fra Norge* cane. Penelope was obedient and attentive to Roger's promptings, and it couldn't have gone any better. When he was finished, Roger's dad was pleased as punch. Neighbor Porky Paulson, who was unaware that the perfectly formed small cyclone of snuff he had just spit on the ground had landed on the toe of Russell's right boot, said, "It looks like your boy brought home the bacon, then."

After watching Roger breeze through the showmanship competition, it was Rodney's turn and he knew everyone was watching. He cocked his head like he had everything in control, but deep down he knew he was going to be put to the test. Roger handed Rodney great-grandpa's *Alt fra Norge* cane, and right from the get-go anything that could go wrong did go wrong. Rodney, who weighed the same as his brother Roger, pulled and pulled and pulled his 130-pound pig, and when he finally got her to move, Petunia slid around like a hog on ice, and headed right for a mud pile. Rodney's adrenaline started to ramp up, and he hit Petunia under the chin so hard he stunned his pig and Petunia laid down in the mud and looked like she was dead. Rodney grabbed a rope and lassoed it around Petunia's neck, but he couldn't budge her. Rodney pulled so hard he fell down in the mud right by Petunia and couldn't get up. Finally, Roger came over and helped Rodney up, and gave him an old rag to wipe off. Roger pulled a small potato from his pocket and Petunia immediately got up. The show was over.

The boys and their dad got in their pickup and went home. Nobody said a word all the way home, except Roger. He pinched his nose, then looked at his brother and said, "You smell barn." Rodney looked at him, and said, "Way to rub it in." The next day they received their showmanship reports and Rodney knew what it would say, so he put it in his pocket and never read it. He was well aware he would be tested again at the county fair, and he knew he had to brush up on his showmanship techniques or his brother would show him up again.

After the county fair was over, Rodney decided he was done with pigs and he would only exhibit wheat and corn. He knew Grandpa Ralph would do the painstaking work of cleaning and sorting the kernels, thus guaranteeing him at least a blue at Achievement Days.

When he was fifteen-years old, he and his brother went to the Crookston Agriculture School. At school, he became interested in equine studies with concentrations in horse rearing, lassoing, roping and stud farming. He spent his summers "playing cowboy," and competed in rodeos all over the Midwest, and even in Wyoming. Three years after he finished high school, it was Yippee Ki-ya for Rodney. He married Pamela Welk, North Dakota's Rodeo Queen with Germans-from-Russia roots, and moved to Western North Dakota to take over his father-in-law's ranch.

Roger studied animal husbandry at the Crookston Ag School, and after high school he started working with his dad on the Rosholt homestead. When he had his ducks in a row and his folks had retired, he married Carol Christianson, a local girl who one year was the local pork queen, and secretary-treasurer of FHA for four years. She was also the sole heiress to a section of land within driving distance of his homestead. It was a marriage made in "hog heaven." They moved to the Rosholt farm, and the fourth generation of Rosholt farmers had begun.

[1]Russell and Shirley were married at the *Trefoldighet* Lutheran Church parsonage on Saturday morning, March 3, 1945. After they went down to Olmstad's Photography Studio to have their wedding photo taken, they went to her parents' home where her mother had prepared a roast beef dinner with all the trimmings for them and their attendants.

[2]At their Silver Wedding Anniversary celebration held at *Trefoldighet* Lutheran Church, Ralph surprised everyone by publicly thanking his wife for helping out with all the milking and getting them through the tough times. Olga, who was big-boned and suffered from phlebitis like her mother-in-law Halvilde, was always the sturdy one when it came to bucking up. She felt foolish that he shared his feelings in front of so many people.

[3]*Halling* is short for the *Halligdal* dance. The "loose dance," as it is often called, involves acrobatics, showing off, and invariably leads to looseness and fighting.

The Last Milking

Russell Rosholt knew in his heart and soul that there is a beginning, middle and an end to everything in life, and tonight was one of those times there would be an ending that wouldn't wind up being a cherished memory. "Yup, Yup,"

he said to Shirley after he had just finished eating supper on a nippy, windy March evening. "Spose, I best get it done."

Russell put on his four-bucklers and barn coat, picked up his milking pails that were sitting by the separator, and started walking to the barn. He had been milking for 45 years and now, just like that, it was going to be over. He was down to two Holsteins—Daisy and Dora, and one Guernsey which he named Delilah.

When he got in the barn, he turned his AM radio on to some milking music. "His girls" were waiting patiently in their stalls. He had decided that for old times' sake he was going to milk by hand, and they wouldn't mind. They knew his touch. He grabbed the three-legged stool that his Grandpa Rollef had made, and put it underneath Daisy. They were smart, loyal cows and they all knew who was milked first, and they never lowed while waiting their turn.

Without the noisy milking machine going, all that was heard were the squirts of milk dropping into the pail. He decided to talk to "his girls" so they wouldn't figure out that something was up.

He said, "I don't know if I ever told you but my Grandma Halvilde was a milkmaid in Norway and would spend her

summers on the Rosholt mountain *seter* milking goats and making cheese. That's where she met Rollef. One day when she was milking he proposed to her and asked her if she would be willing to come to Minnesota with him and milk cows. She said she guessed

222

she could because it didn't matter to her where she milked, or what she milked." So they came.

"The first three milking cows they bought she named Hilda, Signy and Freya after her sisters. How do you like those names? You can be lucky you weren't alive when she was milking. I've heard many stories about her. There wasn't a cow around that would swing a tail at her. Nope, she wasn't afraid of them, and they knew she meant business. They lined up in their stalls and didn't blink an eye when she clamped their stanchions shut. She had a good side though. We always waited on Christmas Eve to eat supper because she spent extra time in the barn giving every animal extra food."

"I think she secretly liked to scare me because she would tell me stories about mean one-eyed trolls, and billy goats that were gruff and would eat me up if I didn't behave. She told me to beware of the *Hulder* women who were born with cowtails and lived in the woods. Once I even told my mother that I was pretty sure Widow Snustad was a *Hulder*."

"It was rumored she even smoked a pipe. Rollef found the pipe one day under the steps and asked her about the pipe. She told him a *Hulder* had left it so he didn't say anymore."

Russell was just finishing up milking Delilah when Tillman Hanson, their hired man, walked into the barn. Tillman said, "Thought I would come by then, and just look around for one last time, if you don't mind." He'd had his share of woes in life with the bottle and with women, but, for years he had been a faithful hired man for the Rosholts' families.

Russell, with his hands on Delilah's udder, squirted Tillman in the face, and said, "I thought you might want a drink." Tillman chuckled and said, "Don't mind if I do, but I got something better," Tillman said as he reached up and pulled out a bottle of cheap Boone Berry Cherry wine from an old tool box. He took a swig, passed it on to Russell, and said, "Here, have a gulp. It's good for the ticker." Russell, who didn't drink alcohol other than communion wine, thought what the heck, and said, "Don't mind if I do, but like Grandma Halvilde always said, what happens in the barn stays in the barn."

Before you knew it the bottle was empty, and Russell and Tilman sat down on a couple of hay bales. Tillman, who always smelled barn, took out his tin of Copenhagen, put a wad in his mouth, handed it to Russell and said, "Here, have a pinch." Russell, who had secretly chewed most of his life but had given it up a couple of years ago because of a suspicious sore on his lip, said "I guess one pinch won't hurt, then."

They sat in silence for a few minutes. Then Russell started talking while he was pointing around the room."Yup, I remember my dad bought more cows right after he bought the Farmall. He said he didn't need our plough horses anymore so he sent them to the glue factory. I was a kid, and that was a tough day," he said as he spit out his Copenhagen. Tillman said, "Well, you've got the harnesses there on the wall which should help. I must admit it was always tough when that rendering truck backed up to the door. Yup, Yup, Yup, a guy never knows."

Russell pointed to the cow bells that were hanging on the wall and said, "Hopefully those will stay put until the barn falls in. Those aren't going to go with the cows tomorrow. I'll make sure of that."

Russell looked around some more. Tillman said, "Here, have another swig." Russell took a big slurp and said, "I never hid a bottle; I left that up to you." Tillman was a little uncomfortable with that comment so he changed the subject.

"My memories in the hayloft go way back to the time I was a young buck. Once I brought a girl upstairs and then didn't know how to handle everything, if you know what I mean. So I chickened out and brought her home. People were hoping during the Depression that your dad would sell it all off and turn the upstairs into a dance hall, but he

was too "Lutheran" to let that ever happen. I don't know if I ever told you, but there are a couple of ghosts hanging out in this barn. I think one of the ghosts is your Grandma Halvilde, and she is probably looking for her pipe. The other one is probably that old neighbor bachelor who used a rope on himself. He did it the day after we had finished loading in all the hay. I went up there just to smell it; you know there's nothing better than the smell of new hay. And there he hung, never could figure out why he didn't use his own barn to do what he thought he needed to do."

Russell who wanted to change the subject pointed to the southwest wall and said, "Just look at all those license plates pounded on the wall. It's quite the history. For a while Grandma Halvilde penned in that area and started raising some chicks. As a young kid I helped her pick the eggs. I didn't like it because as soon as I tried to grab an egg I would get pecked over and over. Then one of her roosters would take after me every time I came through the door. She was tough and told me to get used to it.

Finally, Grandpa Rollef said the barn was getting to look like Noah's Ark and agreed to build her a brooder house.

His barn was his castle, and he said he didn't want a bunch of dumb clucks running around in there ruling the roost. As soon as she got her brooder house, she talked Grandpa into getting a few pigs to put in there. Well, soon she had so many litters of piglets that she penned off part of the horse stalls for them. And now, well, I'm down to three cows and they'll be gone tomorrow. It makes a guy feel kind of useless." Russell took off his barn jacket, hung it on a nail, and said, "Well, I guess I won't need this anymore."

Tillman handed him a couple of Sen-sens, cleared his throat, got up from his hay bale and said, "Well, best be going. I'll be over bright and early to milk them before I get them ready for the auction."

After Tillman left, Russell went over to pat Daisy, Dora and Delilah for one last time. He said, "Tomorrow you'll have a new home. Grandma Halvilde always said all things must come to an end. Yup, I guess she was right."

The Auction

A few days after the last of the *fattigman* had been eaten
and Christmas was a memory, Shirley knew they had to get
down to business and start sorting, packing, and throwing so
they could get ready for their auction which was scheduled
for the third week in March.

This was no easy task because she had three generations
of Rosholt stuff to go through. The first two generations of
Rosholts all died at the homestead so they never moved,
never sorted anything and never had an auction. When she
and Russell moved in, anything that didn't work, they didn't

want or they wouldn't use, they stored in the attic and in buildings all over the farmstead. She was relieved when her son, Roger, who was going to be moving into the homestead house, told her to hang on to the stuff that was brought over from the old country.

Sorting the volumes of papers, magazines and reading material tested Shirley to the core. She knew it said in the good book that there was "a time to keep and a time to throw away", but Norwegian-Lutheran guilt took over when it came to throwing devotional books, tracts, and Grandma Olga's sermon notes that were written in Norwegian at the time she was "Reading for the Minister." Sometimes Shirley became so frustrated she just wanted to chuck the whole kit and caboodle into the burning barrel, but she always came to her senses. Finally, two days before the auction she was ready.

The auctioneer and his team had been there for a couple of days, and Russell helped them line up the machinery, the surplus milking stuff and anything else that was to be sold. The morning of the auction, the team was there at 6:00 a.m. to move the household stuff out of the house and onto tables that were set up in the yard.

After Shirley had fed Russell breakfast, she went out to the yard to look around.

As she was looking over her "life history," she became a little irked thinking about Widow Snustad, Mrs. Elmer Stordahl, Tekla Torkelson and Mrs. Nels Lillegaard. She knew they would be driving out together to snoop and rummage through her stuff and pick up things and smell them. She knew they had no intentions of bidding on anything, and they would hang around and wait to see who bid on various things, and what kind of deal they got on them.

She had a pang of guilt and a change of heart while looking at her stuff and quickly grabbed the arm and back covers that Grandma Halvilde had crocheted to cover her davenport. She brought them back into the house along with some old bed pillows that needed re-ticking and an old metal meat grinder.

The auction was starting at 9:30 a.m. sharp, and she knew that the *Trefoldighet* Ladies Aid would be there about 7:30 a.m. to set up the lunch stand. She also knew this would be a tough day for Russell. He was a little cranky in the days leading up to the auction, so she just stayed out of his way and pretended like everything was normal.

The farmers, young and old, started coming around 8:00 a.m. Some of them had been there the day before to scout it out. The younger grown up ones, like Dougie Johnson, lined up to get their bidding numbers, and the old ones just came to watch the auctioneer and his helpers who were perched on a hay wagon trying to get the bids up while working the crowd. They also came to be of some kind of moral support for Russell, even though they just talked about the weather to him. The old farmers stood in the same area, and talked freely among themselves about other recent auctions, the high price of land and seed, the low price of wheat, who had recently bought more land and had taken on more than they could chew, and how many of them might be squeezed out shortly. Ole Arnegaard, a local whose family had lost their farm in the Depression, said, "None of these young bucks lived through the Depression and tough times. They buy like there's no tomorrow, and they have no idea what's coming down the road."

After the auction was over, and the last pickup had pulled out of the driveway, Russell, Shirley, Roger and Carol went into the house. Shirley felt tears running down her cheeks and quickly beat it to the bathroom so the men wouldn't see her. Good grief, she said to herself as she washed her face. Shirley straightened up and went to the kitchen to start supper for her men who were talking and sitting by the table waiting. Russell said, "I can't figure out for the life of me why my 28-foot hay bale elevator didn't fetch more." "Well," Roger said, "I'm not surprised. Nobody stores hay in their upstairs barn in this day and age. We're just lucky we got rid of it and didn't have to park it out in the grove. There's enough stuff to pack up the way it is."

They only had a few weeks to get all the packing done for

their move to town. Shirley knew she had saved too much stuff to bring along, but she would cross that bridge when she came to it. She told Russell she was bringing along the old cream separator and plunking it in the front lawn to use as a petunia pot. He shook his head and said, "It's a good thing we're not Catholic or you'd also be dragging that old iron bathtub to use as a shelter for a Mary statue."

Russell was no better. He had hoarded his treasures like a squirrel getting ready for winter, and insisted upon saving and bringing with all his old cancelled checks, boxes of yearly statistics of pork prices, cans of bent nails, horseshoes and a good size pile of scrap lumber.

Finally they were finished, and their new life in town was

about to start. Shirley kept her trusted chokecherry picking pails and a few other things out at the farm. Russell decided all his old license plates that he had pounded on the wall would stay put and be safe. They were confident that Roger knew better than to throw them. Even the dog stayed and would be safe and sound in the Rosholt barn.

Retirement – Rosholt Style

Visitors at the Rosholt home in town

After Russell and Shirley moved into their ranch house in Herringdal, they settled into a routine without much fuss. They didn't travel much, but they looked forward to their annual trip to the Badlands where they visited Rodney and his family, and taking their yearly trip to the Valley City Winter Show.

They had traveled to the Valley City Winter Show for their honeymoon and stayed at the Kindred Hotel. They got to hear Peggy Lee singing "Ghost Rider's in the Sky" when they were at the winter shows in '55, and never forgot it.

Shirley had enough space in town to plant a big flower garden filled with gladiolus. She was on the altar guild committee at *Trefoldiget* Lutheran Church so they came in handy. She kept her "canning garden" out on the homestead. She would can so many pints and quarts of everything that one day Russell said, "I think you've canned enough to feed everyone in Fish County for a year." She was also secretary-treasurer of her homemaker's club, and just generally never sat down except to watch "Party Line" and "Lawrence Welk" on their new Philco TV they bought when they moved to town.

Russell kept busy tinkering around, greasing squeaky doors, changing blown fuses and sorting and straightening bent nails. Religiously, he recorded the daily price of pork for his son Roger. He was on the *Trefoldighet* Cemetery Board, and once a year he made an appearance at the annual meeting. He also showed up at every local farm auction, but he never bought anything. His ticker was acting up a little bit but he never told anyone. He just took a couple of naps every day and hoped everything would iron itself out.

With his Grandson Richard, he would sit for hours by the kitchen table, meticulously helping him to separate and pull out the good kernels of wheat that Richard would use for his 4-H country fair entry. Every year, Richard knew his grandpa would retell him the same story about the time his dad Roger and Uncle Rodney were showing their pigs, Penelope and Petunia, and how everything went south for Rodney.

Russell would get a little antsy when spring planting time came around, and couldn't wait to go out to the homestead to help with the farming and breathe in the good smell of dirt. Every year when planting time rolled around, he would say to Shirley, "It was so good to be back on the Allis again."

They've Earned a Good Rest

One day in May, Russell succumbed to a heart attack while he was helping Roger with the spring cultivating. He was found slumped over and leaning against the back tractor tire with his lunch pail opened. He had a "termos" cup in his right hand, a summer sausage sandwich in the other hand, and a sugar lump between his upper and lower plates. They quickly realized, his ticker had stopped and he was gone.

It was a little lonely for Shirley, but she was a capable woman who adjusted herself to widowhood by just keeping busy. As she told her friend Emogene Flestrud, "It is what it is. They say life is like a roll of toilet paper. The closer you get to the end, the faster it goes."

She passed the time away by darning socks and watching WDAY's "Party Line" program which was co-hosted by Lois Leppart. Shirley thought Lois was as fancy as Norma Zimmer, Lawrence Welk's Champagne Lady. She kept busy cleaning and attending Ladies Aid and homemaker's club activities. She continued to can pickles up until her mid-eighties.

The year she turned 85, her memory was slipping pretty good. One day she forgot she had filled the pressure cooker with pint jars of crabapple pickles, and things went from bad to worse. She couldn't see the steam coming out of the cooker because of her cataracts. She didn't have her hearing aids in so she couldn't hear the pressure cooker's warning whistle. It was a good thing she wasn't in the kitchen when the whole kit and caboodle exploded. There were broken pint jars of crabapples all over the counters, stove and floor. A couple of hot crabapples had flown across the counter and landed on her terrycloth mixer cover and burned a big hole in it. There were black burn marks on the linoleum floor, the linoleum counter top and the rag rug in front of the stove. The copper Jell-O molds, which were hung on the wall behind her counter, were dripping with hot crabapple syrup as was her "Oh Lord of all Pots and Pans and Things" plaster-of-paris kitchen prayer plaque. Another hot crabapple had flown into the bacon grease tin which was sitting on the stove and started on fire. The kitchen looked like a war zone, and when Shirley saw it, she went into action. She grabbed a big white dishtowel and wet it to smother out the flames. Just to make sure the fire was all out, she dumped a whole box of Morton salt on it. "When it rains, it pours."

Shortly after that incident, Roger bought her an aqua-blue trailer house, parked it on the homestead and moved her in so they could keep track of her. One day she just slept away in her recliner.

Shirley was buried next to Russell in the Rosholt family plot located in the northeast corner of the *Trefoldighet* Lutheran Church Cemetery. The Rosholt headstone is facing the homestead. *This is most certainly true.*

Faithful Lutheran church sexton holding the cemetery plat map

About the Authors

Janet Letnes Martin

Janet Letnes Martin grew up in Hillsboro, ND where the words "Norwegian and Lutheran" were synonymous. It was no surprise she graduated from Augsburg College, in Minneapolis, MN and married Neil Martin, a 100% Scandinavian-Lutheran man from Newfolden, MN.

Janet started writing books in 1983. She had authored four books, co-authored three books with Allen Todnem, and one with her sister, Ilene Lorenz, before she teamed up to write and perform with a college friend, Suzann Nelson. Suzann and Janet have written ten books relating to their Norwegian-Lutheran-rural background. Their book, Growing Up Lutheran, What Does This Mean? won the Minnesota Book Award for humor, the Minnesota Independent Publisher's Award, and is the inspiration for all six "Church Basement Ladies" musicals.

In 2007, Janet 'switched gears' and teamed up with author/artist, David W. Cook II to write a fabulous, humorous, book entitled, Lemonade for the Lawnboy: The Executives' Wives' Cookbook Committee. The book was turned into the musical entitled "Lemonade for the Lawnboy" – The Musical.

Janet has been speaking to churches and organizations for 30 years. She often teams up with her co-author Suzann Nelson to perform a comedy routine entitled "Those Lutheran Ladies."

Janet lives in Hastings, MN and is the mother of three daughters, 5 granddaughters, and one grandson. Her husband, Neil passed away in 2006.

Order Information:
Janet can be contacted at lutheranladies@aol.com or Caragana Press, Box 274, Hastings, MN 55033 or by phone at 1-800-797-4319.

SUZANN NELSON

As half of the knowledgeable, funny, 100 percent Norwegian-Lutheran duo, "Those Lutheran Ladies," Suzann Nelson could just list her name under Janet Martin's and type ditto. Names and a few places might differ, but their histories are similar and often identical — from the month and year they were baptized and confirmed Lutheran to the day, in 1968, when they graduated from the same Norwegian Lutheran college.

Nelson began life as a Johnson on a "Noah's Ark" farm — two cows, two pigs, two chickens and two brothers — close to where the Kensington Runestone was found. After graduating high school in Evansville, MN, Suzann boarded a train for the nearest Sin City, Minneapolis. She graduated with a Scandinavian Studies major from Augsburg College where she also met her 100% Norwegian Lutheran husband, Ron, and someone named Janet Letnes — both decent, wholesome folks who had grown up in North Dakota eating cream on bread.

After further study at the Universities of MN and Oslo, Suzann directed Concordia College's Norwegian Language Village, *Skogfjorden*, and in off seasons had three-piece suit jobs where she dabbled in government, public policy work and in putting on pantyhose.

Eventually, Suzann and Ron moved to Grand Rapids, MN where they raised their two 100% Norwegian-Lutheran daughters, Senja and Siri.

Now a mother-in-law, widow, and owner of an online business, Suzann spends her days and nights pondering ways to pay off her mortgage, looking for misplaced things, being fascinated by four grandchildren, and ironing used wrapping paper.

Order Information:
Rural Route Bookstore www.ruralroutebookstore.com